Where do I go for answers to my travel questions?

What's the best and easiest way to plan and book my trip?

frommers.travelocity.com

Frommer's, the travel guide leader, has teamed up with **Travelocity.com,** the leader in online travel, to bring you an in-depth, easy-to-use resource designed to help you plan and book your trip online.

At **frommers.travelocity.com**, you'll find free online updates about your destination from the experts at Frommer's plus the outstanding travel planning and purchasing features of Travelocity.com. Travelocity.com provides reservations capabilities for 95 percent of all airline seats sold, more than 47,000 hotels, and over 50 car rental companies. In addition, Travelocity.com offers more than 2,000 exciting vacation and cruise packages. Travelocity.com puts you in complete control of your travel planning with these and other great features:

> **Expert travel guidance from Frommer's** - over 150 writers reporting from around the world!
>
> **Best Fare Finder** - an interactive calendar tells you when to travel to get the best airfare
>
> **Fare Watcher** - we'll track airfare changes to your favorite destinations
>
> **Dream Maps** - a mapping feature that suggests travel opportunities based on your budget
>
> **Shop Safe Guarantee** - 24 hours a day / 7 days a week live customer service, and more!

Whether traveling on a tight budget, looking for a quick weekend getaway, or planning the trip of a lifetime, Frommer's guides and Travelocity.com will make your travel dreams a reality. You've bought the book, now book the trip!

Frommer's®

Other Great Guides for Your Trip:

Frommer's San Antonio & Austin

Frommer's Texas

Frommer's USA

Here's what the critics say about Frommer's:

"Amazingly easy to use. Very portable, very complete."

♦

"The only mainstream guide to list specific prices. The Walter Cronkite of guidebooks—with all that implies."

♦

"Complete, concise, and filled with useful information."

♦

"Hotel information is close to encyclopedic."

P O R T A B L E

Houston
1st Edition

by David Baird

with Don and Barb Laine

Hungry Minds™

Best-Selling Books • Digital Downloads • e-Books • Answer Networks
e-Newsletters • Branded Web Sites • e-Learning

New York, NY • Cleveland, OH • Indianapolis, IN

ABOUT THE AUTHORS

Born and bred in Houston, **David Baird** (chapters 1–9) now lives in Austin where he writes, edits, researches, and translates for a variety of projects. He has contributed to *Frommer's Texas* and *Frommer's Mexico*.

Residents of northern New Mexico since 1970, **Don and Barb Laine** (chapters 1, 2, and 10) have traveled extensively throughout the West, spending as much time as possible in the outdoors, particularly the Gulf of Mexico and the Rocky Mountains. They have authored or contributed to *Frommer's Texas, Frommer's Colorado, Frommer's Utah,* and *Frommer's National Parks of the American West.*

Published by:

HUNGRY MINDS, INC.

909 Third Ave.
New York, NY 10022
www.frommers.com

ISBN 0-7645-6453-6
ISSN 1532-9976

Editor: Myka Carroll
Production Editor: Cara L. Buitron
Photo Editor: Richard Fox
Design by Michele Laseau
Cartographer: Roberta Stockwell
Production by Hungry Minds Indianapolis Production Services

SPECIAL SALES

For general information on Hungry Minds' products and services, please contact our Customer Care department; within the U.S. at 800-762-2974, outside the U.S. at 317-572-3993 or fax 317-572-4002. For sales inquiries and reseller information, including discounts, bulk sales, customized editions, and premium sales, please contact our Customer Care department at 800-434-3422.

Manufactured in the United States of America

5 4 3 2 1

Contents

List of Maps

An Invitation to the Reader

In researching this book, we discovered many wonderful places—hotels, restaurants, shops, and more. We're sure you'll find others. Please tell us about them, so we can share the information with your fellow travelers in upcoming editions. If you were disappointed with a recommendation, we'd love to know that, too. Please write to:

Frommer's Portable Houston, 1st Edition
Hungry Minds, Inc.
909 Third Avenue
New York, NY 10022

An Additional Note

Please be advised that travel information is subject to change at any time—and this is especially true of prices. We, therefore, suggest that you write or call ahead for confirmation when making your travel plans. The authors, editors, and publisher cannot be held responsible for the experiences of readers while traveling. Your safety is important to us, however, so we encourage you to stay alert and be aware of your surroundings. Keep a close eye on cameras, purses, and wallets, all favorite targets of thieves and pickpockets.

What the Symbols Mean
✪ Frommer's Favorites

Our favorite places and experiences—outstanding for quality, value, or both.

The following abbreviations are used for credit cards:

AE	American Express	JCB	Japan Credit Bank
CB	Carte Blanche	MC	MasterCard
DC	Diners Club	V	Visa
DISC	Discover		

Find Frommer's Online

www.frommers.com offers up-to-the-minute listings on almost 200 cities around the globe—including the latest bargains and candid, personal articles updated daily by Arthur Frommer himself. No other website offers such comprehensive and timely coverage of the world of travel.

The Best of Houston & the Gulf Coast

*H*ouston, the largest city in Texas (and the fourth most populated city in the United States), is the heart of the nation's oil and gas industry. Although not a primary tourist destination (you're more likely to come here to close a business deal), Houston offers an abundance of attractions, including numerous museums, performing arts such as the city's excellent symphony orchestra, and a variety of outdoor activities. Here you'll find NASA's Johnson Space Center, which has made Houston famous and is the city's most popular attraction; and the Astrodome—billed originally as "the eighth wonder of the world"—the first of the domed sports stadiums. Nearby, Galveston combines small-town easiness with a good mix of museums and children's activities, plus its beaches. East Texas, the area of the state that borders Louisiana from the coastal cities north to where the state meets Arkansas, has wonderful national forests, state parks, rivers, and lakes, and is a destination for anglers and other outdoor recreationists.

The Gulf Coast is where you find the state's ocean—the Gulf of Mexico—and if, as the saying goes, "Life's a Beach," this is life. In addition to the usual beach activities of swimming, sunbathing, beachcombing, boating, and even some surfing (okay, it's no Hawaii, but you *can* surf here), the Texas Gulf Coast is probably the nation's top bird-watching region, and also offers superb fishing opportunities. There are also some good museums and a surprisingly active art scene.

1 The Best Luxury & Historic Hotels

• **The Four Seasons Houston Center** (☎ 800/332-3442 or 713/650-1300): Lots of space to stretch out and lots of service so you don't have to stretch too far. This hotel surpasses all others in amenities and services, and has the best fine dining restaurant in downtown Houston. And only a few blocks away is the city's theater district and nightlife center. See chapter 4.

- **Omni Corpus Christi Hotel** (☎ **800/843-6664** or 361/887-1600): The two towers of the Omni overlook Corpus Christi Bay, and the floor-to-ceiling windows of the 20-story Bayfront Tower offer spectacular views of the Gulf, particularly from its upper floors. In the lobby are several large sailing-ship models, and all units have private balconies. Pamper yourself with a massage from the in-house massage therapist or relax in the whirlpool. Then have dinner in their Republic of Texas Bar & Grill. See chapter 10.

- **Radisson Resort South Padre Island** (☎ **800/333-3333** or 956/761-6511): From the high-ceilinged lobby to the beautiful landscaping around the swimming pools, this Radisson spells luxury. Many rooms have grand views of the ocean, and everything is at your fingertips. See chapter 10.

2 The Best Bed and Breakfasts & Small Hotels

- **La Colombe d'Or** (Houston; ☎ **713/524-7999**): Have a four-course French dinner served in your suite's separate dining room. Service is very personal, and with only five suites and one penthouse, there's no way you will get lost in the shuffle. See chapter 4.

- **Lancaster Hotel** (Houston; ☎ **800/231-0336** or 713/228-9500): Personal service, charming rooms, and great location are the keys to this hotel's success. If there's one hotel that makes having a car unnecessary in Houston, this is it. Within a block of the symphony, the opera, the theater, the ballet, and a multiplex cinema, and within a couple blocks more of several restaurants and bars, you have the best part of the city at your feet. See chapter 4.

Houston's Best Hotel Bargain

Grant Palm Court Inn (☎ **800/255-8904** or 713/668-8000) is a competitive economy hotel business; rarely do we come across a motel in this category with such a marked price advantage. Attractive, clean rooms, well-kept grounds, and a convenient location that's not on some ugly freeway real estate all make this a great pick. Throw in a free continental breakfast, pool, and hot tub and you'll need to pinch yourself. See chapter 4.

Houston's Best Restaurant

No fussy French nouvelle here, and no boring steak and potatoes either: **Mark's** (☎ **713/523-3800**) manages to serve up dishes that can satisfy at some deep subconscious level while they fulfill our eternal quest for something new. This is the new American cooking as it should be performed. See chapter 5.

- **George Blucher House** (Corpus Christi; ☎ **866/884-4884** or 361/884-4884): This wonderful B&B combines the ambience of an elegant historic home—it was built in 1904—with modern amenities. Breakfasts are served by candlelight; and you're just across the street from a prime bird-watching area. See chapter 10.

3 The Best Mexican & Tex-Mex Restaurants

- **Fiesta Loma Linda** (Houston; ☎ **713/924-6074**): You can scour the border a long time before coming up with an old-fashioned Tex-Mex joint like this one. The restaurant even has its own special tortilla maker for producing the puffed up tortillas used in certain Tex-Mex specialties. See chapter 5.
- **Recio's** (Corpus Christi; ☎ **361/888-4040**): South Texas is littered with *taquerias* (restaurants that specialize in *taquitos*—similar to a burrito but folded) and this is among the best. Locally owned and operated by Robert and Minerva Recio, this justly popular restaurant serves homemade cooked-to-order food in a pleasant, casual atmosphere. See chapter 10.

4 The Best Parks & Gardens

- **Bayou Bend** (Houston): The now-deceased owner of Bayou Bend designed several formal gardens and beautifully landscaped grounds on the 14 acres that surround her mansion. They are delightful to visit, especially in the spring and early summer when the azaleas are blooming. See chapter 6.
- **Corpus Christi Botanical Gardens:** This series of gardens along Oso Creek offers a refreshing escape from the city. The rose garden, completed in 2000, contains some 300 roses in a tranquil setting of arbors, trellises, and benches. See chapter 10.

5   The Best Travel Experiences

- **USS *Lexington* Museum on the Bay** (Corpus Christi): Exploring this huge World War II–era aircraft carrier offers non-naval people the opportunity to get an idea of what it was like to live for months at a time in the claustrophobic conditions of such a limited area. In addition to sleeping, dining, and cooking areas, the ship provided a hospital, rec room, and, of course, numerous necessary working areas. See chapter 10.

- **Aransas National Wildlife Refuge** (Rockport): A mecca for birders, with some 400 species sited here, the refuge is also home to a variety of frogs and other amphibians, plus snakes, turtles, lizards, and numerous mammals. But Aransas has become famous for being the main winter home of the near-extinct whooping crane, the tallest bird in America—5 feet tall with a 7-foot wingspan. See chapter 10.

6   The Best Museums

- **The Menil Collection** (Houston): One of the great private collections of the world, it could very well have ended up in Paris or New York, but was graciously bestowed by the collectors on their adopted city. To experience the Menil is pure delight; very little comes between the viewer and the art, some of which includes works by many of the 20th-century masters, classical works from the ancients, and tribal art from around the world. See chapter 6.

- **Museum of Fine Arts Houston:** With the recent addition of the Audrey Jones Beck Building, the Fine Arts museum has doubled its exhibition space and has especially put its collection of impressionist and baroque art in the best possible light. The museum also has several satellite facilities and attracts major touring exhibitions. See chapter 6.

- **Space Center Houston:** Always the most popular attraction in the city, NASA's Space Center Houston is a joint effort powered by NASA technology and Disney know-how. It is the epitome of interactive display and simulation that manages to interest both kids and parents. During your visit, you can check out what's going on at the Johnson Space Center through a tram ride with video feeds. See chapter 6.

- **The Center for the Arts & Sciences** (Brazosport): One of those rare entities that does a whole lot of things exceptionally well, The Center includes a terrific natural history museum, a delightful, small planetarium, an attractive art gallery, two theaters for a variety of performing arts events, and a nature trail. See chapter 10.

7 The Best Beaches and Places for Fishing & Water Sports

- **East Texas** has many lakes that attract the attention of anglers far and wide, partly because of the beautiful pine forests that border these lakes, and partly because of all the record-size largemouth bass that have been caught here. See chapter 8.
- **Galveston** beaches may not enjoy the reputation of those along the South Texas coast, but they have something those beaches don't: the lovely town of Galveston, with its great restaurants, and its fascinating historic district, not to mention a seawall that makes for enjoyable strolling, biking, and skating. See chapter 9.
- **Mustang Island State Park** (Corpus Christi): This barrier island has more than 5 miles of wide, sandy beach, with fine sand, few rocks and broken shells, and almost enough waves for surfing. It also offers excellent fishing from jetties. A 48-site campground has water and electric hookups, and there is almost unlimited beach camping. The park is one of the most popular of Texas state parks and is especially busy on summer weekends. See chapter 10.
- **The Gulf Side of South Padre Island:** Fine white sand and warm water lapping at your toes—what more do you want? Although the shore is lined with hotels and condos, the beaches are public and open to everyone. See chapter 10.
- **Freeport** (Brazosport): For a small town, Freeport certainly has a lot of fish—and charter boats from which to catch them. Or, you can try from the shore, beach, pier, or jetty. Deep-sea fishing trips are also popular. See chapter 10.

2

Planning a Trip to Houston

*S*ituated on a flat, near featureless Gulf Coast plain, Houston sprawls from its center in vast tracts of subdivisions, freeways, office parks, and shopping malls. In undisturbed areas you'll find grasslands (often marshy) to the south and woods to the north. Meandering across this plain are several bayous on whose banks cypress and southern magnolia trees chance to grow. Many visitors, imagining the Texas landscape as it is usually drawn—barren and treeless—are surprised by such green surroundings.

Houston is the fourth most-populated city in the United States. If we compare the populations of greater metro areas rather than cities, then Houston ranks only 10th, with far fewer people than such urban centers as the San Francisco Bay area. Yet (and this is the telling fact), in geographical size Houston ranks second. The city is more than half as large as the state of Rhode Island. In the past few years, however, Houstonians changed their minds about living far out in the suburbs, deciding that it would be nicer to live closer to the city's main attractions; the main thrust of residential construction has shifted away from the suburban expansion and towards the downtown and inner-city areas. Townhouses in the central part of town are going up at a furious rate, and lofts, condos, and apartments are now a major part of downtown construction.

If you had to characterize Houston in a single word or phrase, it would be "wide open." Economically and socially, Houston is fluid without a rigidly structured society or a controlling business elite. This inclusiveness has brought a steady flow of newcomers to the city from other parts of the nation and from abroad, for whom the city represents the land of opportunity. For Houston, this influx of people has meant a growing cosmopolitanism. Restaurants and specialty shops have sprung up that cater to the new immigrant populations,

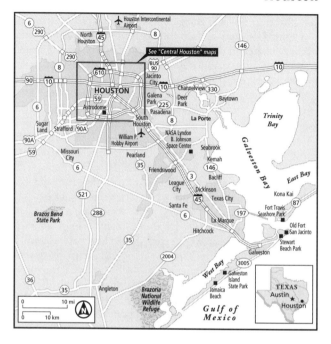

and throughout the city, in some of the most unlikely places you'll see exotic temples and churches—Taoist, Buddhist, Hindu, Islamic, Russian Orthodox—built much like they would be back in the mother country.

Many of these immigrants have a certain laissez-faire attitude toward government that is perfectly in keeping with native beliefs. Houstonians have always displayed an inherent dislike for being told what to do. Among urban planners, Houston is famous (or infamous) as the only major U.S. city that doesn't have zoning, allowing the market to determine land use instead. But now, as the city struggles with an air pollution problem that has placed it at the top of the list of the nation's worst offenders, the local government must consider regulations and ordinances to keep the city habitable. It is almost a crisis of fundamental truths as the much-loved philosophy of no regulation clashes with the hard reality of polluted air.

But this crisis isn't going to provoke a lot of hand-wringing among Houstonians, who are generally an exuberant and good-natured bunch. When the headlines appeared about Houston surpassing Los Angeles in having the dirtiest air in the nation, several people sardonically hoisted signs bragging about beating L.A. This good humor, exuberance, and love of hyperbole can be found in many things during the course of a visit to the city, including local speech, gestures, and mannerisms—and in the city's architecture. This is, after all the home of the Astrodome, billed originally as "the eighth wonder of the world," the first of the domed stadiums. It is also home to more recent buildings where Houston developers have commissioned architects who weren't shy about making bold and even playful statements—thus you have a skyscraper downtown that is crowned with a Mayan pyramid, another where the architect wryly used the architectural elements of gothic churches for a bank building, and a pair of towers in the Medical Center that unmistakably represent two giant syringes. And these are but a few examples of all the fun being had in the area of the arts where Houston is taken quite seriously, thanks to the city's excellent symphony orchestra, its highly respected ballet and opera companies, and a dynamic theater scene that few cities can equal in quantity or quality. Add to this some tip-top museums, and you won't be lacking for entertainment choices.

1 Visitor Information & Money

VISITOR INFORMATION

For advance information, try ☎ 800/4-HOUSTON or www. houston-guide.com. Other Web sites you might find helpful are **www.houstonchronicle.com** and **www.houstonpress. com**. The *Houston Chronicle* is the city's only daily newspaper; the *Houston Press* is a weekly tabloid freebie that does a good job of covering the week's events in the city and has a large entertainment section.

MONEY

Like almost everywhere else in the United States, credit cards are the most common form of payment for practically everything throughout Houston, and are accepted—even preferred—in many hotels, restaurants, shops, attractions, and major grocery stores. In general, traveler's checks (in U.S. dollars) are also welcome, but be aware that smaller businesses, and especially those in small towns, may not be able to cash traveler's checks or even American currency in large denominations (over $50). ATMs (automated teller machines) for all the major national networks are practically everywhere, including many supermarkets and discount stores. If you can't find one, call ☎ **800/THE-PLUS.**

2 When to Go

Houston is at the tail end of a large belt of natural forest coming down through east Texas, and the climate is much the same as coastal Louisiana and Mississippi—warm and humid with ample rainfall.

Houston's Average High/Low Temperatures & Precipitation

	Jan	Feb	Mar	Apr	May	June	July	Aug	Sept	Oct	Nov	Dec
High °F	62	65	75	79	85	90	92	92	88	81	72	65
Low °F	43	45	53	61	67	73	75	75	71	61	53	45
Precip.	3.2	2.8	2.4	2.5	4.4	5.3	3.9	3.8	4.9	3.4	3.6	3.0

HOUSTON & THE GULF COAST CALENDAR OF EVENTS

February

- **Houston Livestock Show and Rodeo,** Houston. Billed as the largest event of its kind, the Rodeo includes all the usual events like bull riding and calf roping, plus performances by famous country-and-western artists. A parade downtown kicks off the celebration. Call ☎ **713/791-9000.** Mid-February.
- **Mardi Gras,** Galveston. The city's biggest party of the year, with parades, masked balls, and a live-entertainment district around the Strand. Call ☎ **888/425-4753.** February into March.

April

- **International Festival,** Houston. This festival highlights the culture, food, music, and heritage of a different country every year. The organizers work closely with the local immigrant group and consulate of the designated country to bring musicians and artists to the event. Call ☎ **713/926-6368.** Mid- to late April.

- **Art Car Parade and Ball,** Houston. The parade of decorated cars is marvelous and hilarious and attracts participants from around the country. The ball—held in a large downtown parking garage—is guaranteed to be a spirited event. Call ☎ **713/926-6368.** Mid- to late April.
- **Windsurfing Blowout,** South Padre Island. For some 20 years, increasing numbers of windsurfers have been attending this jamboree. Call ☎ **800/678-6232** or 361/561-2000. Late April to early May.

June

- **C-101 Sand Castle Sculptures,** Corpus Christi. Calling all S.O.B.s (Sons of the Beach, that is). Bring your talents and imaginations and dig in. Call ☎ **800/678-6232** or 361/561-2000. Early June.
- ✪ **American Institute of Architects Sandcastle Competition,** Galveston. More than 70 architectural and engineering firms from around the state build sand castles and sand sculptures, taking this pastime to new heights. Construction must be completed between 11am and 4pm. Call ☎ **713/520-0155.** First weekend in June.
- **Juneteenth Festival,** Houston. Celebration of the day slavery was abolished in Texas with blues, jazz, gospel music, and a variety of events. Call ☎ **713/284-8352.** Weekend nearest June 19.

July

- **Texas International Fishing Tournament (TIFT),** South Padre Island. This 5-day event has been promoting friendly fishing competition and wholesome family fun for more than 60 years. Call ☎ **800/678-6232** or 361/561-2000. Late July into early August.

September

- **Fiestas Patrias,** Houston. One of the largest community-sponsored parades in the Southwest celebrating Mexico's independence from Spain. Houston's several Ballet Folklórico troupes twirl their way through downtown streets in a pageantry of color and traditional Mexican music. Call ☎ **713/926-2636.** Mid-September.
- **Texaco-Havoline Grand Prix,** Houston. A section of downtown is closed off to create a 1¾-mile course for CART Indy-style cars. As the air fills with the high pitch of racing engines, many of Houston's boldest drivers enact their racing fantasies on the city's freeways. Call ☎ **713/739-7272.** Late September.

- **Bayfest!,** Corpus Christi. This huge festival fills Shoreline Drive from I-37 down to Bayfront Park with music, games, food, arts and crafts, and fireworks over the bay. Call ☎ **800/678-6232** or 361/561-2000. Late September.

October
- **Longest Causeway Run & Wellness Walk,** South Padre Island. Annual 2½-mile race across the Queen Isabella Causeway. Call ☎ **800/678-6232** or 361/561-2000. Early October.
- **Texas Jazz Festival,** Corpus Christi. This free festival attracts hundreds of musicians. Call ☎ **800/678-6232** or 361/561-2000. Mid- to late October.
- **Wings Over Houston Airshow,** Houston. This thrilling event usually features a display of current military aircraft and performances of aerial acrobatics. Call ☎ **281/531-9461.** Mid- to late October.

November
- **South Padre Island Kite Festival,** South Padre Island. What could be more fun than flying a kite above blue waters? Or prettier to watch? For all those still young at heart. Call ☎ **800/678-6232** or 361/561-2000. Early November.

December
- **Harbor Lights Celebration,** Corpus Christi. The harbor is decked out for the holidays. Call ☎ **800/678-6232** or 361/561-2000. First weekend in December.
- **Dickens on The Strand,** Galveston. A street party in the historic district of the city where revelers dress up in Victorian costume to celebrate. There are parades, performers, street vendors, and lots of entertainment. Call ☎ **409/765-7834.** First weekend in December.

3 Health & Insurance

STAYING HEALTHY

Those traveling to Houston generally need take no extra health precautions than they would at home. Before starting out, check your medical insurance policy to be certain you're covered away from home; if not, purchase a special traveler's policy, available from travel agents, insurance agents, and travel clubs. Companies specializing in medical care include **MEDEX International** (☎ **888/MEDEX-00** or 410/453-6300; www.medexassist.com), and **Travel Assistance**

International (☎ **800/821-2828**). It's useful to carry a medical-insurance identification card with you at all times.

INSURANCE

Besides being prepared for medical emergencies, it's wise to carry insurance to cover you in case of an accident, loss of personal possessions such as luggage and cameras (this may be included in your homeowner's or renter's policy), or trip cancellation (especially if you've prepaid a large portion of your vacation expenses). If you are a motorist, be sure to carry proof of automobile liability insurance, and be certain that your policy includes protection from uninsured motorists.

Among the reputable issuers of travel insurance are: **Access America** (☎ 800/284-8300), **Travel Guard International** (☎ 800/826-1300), **Travel Insured International Inc.** (☎ 800/243-3174), or **Travelex Insurance Services** (☎ 800/228-9792).

4 Tips for Travelers with Special Needs

FOR TRAVELERS WITH DISABILITIES

Travelers with physical disabilities should find Texas relatively easy to get around. Although some older hotels and restaurants may not be wheelchair-accessible, newer properties, plus most major parks and historical monuments, are. To be safe, it's best to call ahead to make sure facilities are suitable.

Access-Able Travel Source (www.access-able.com) is a comprehensive database of travel agents who specialize in helping travelers with disabilities; it's also a clearinghouse for information about accessible destinations around the world. Another good resource for travelers with any type of disability is **Mobility International USA,** P.O. Box 10767, Eugene, OR 97440 (☎ **541/343-1284** voice and TDD; www.miusa.org), a nonprofit organization involved in promoting travel awareness for people who have difficulty in getting around. The organization publishes *A World of Options,* a 658-page book of resources for travelers with disabilities, covering everything from biking trips to scuba outfitters ($35).

If you're planning to visit the national parks, monuments, historic sites, and wildlife refuges, you can get the federal government's **Golden Access Passport,** available free at all visitor centers. This lifetime pass is issued to any U.S. citizen or permanent resident who is medically certified as disabled or blind. The pass permits free entry and gives a 50% discount on park-service campgrounds and activities (but not on those offered by private concessions).

With 24-hour notice, **Amtrak** (☎ **800/USA-RAIL**) will provide porter service, special seating, and a discount on most runs.

FOR GAY & LESBIAN TRAVELERS

In general, gay and lesbian travelers will find they are treated just like any other visitors. Even though the state does have a decidedly conservative bent, Texans generally have a "live and let live" attitude. A gay and lesbian-oriented weekly newspaper, *Texas Triangle* (☎ **512/476-0576;** www.txtriangle.com), is available at newsstands with state and national news, features, nightlife, a calendar of events, and classified ads. Information is also available from the **Lesbian/Gay Rights Lobby of Texas,** P.O. Box 2340, Austin, TX 78768 (☎ **512/ 474-5475;** www.outtexas.org); and you'll find links to a number of websites at **www.lbgsa.org/links/local.htm**.

FOR SENIORS

Many hotels and motels offer discounts to senior citizens (especially if you're carrying an AARP card; see below), and an increasing number of restaurants, attractions, and public transportation systems do so as well. **Train travelers** 62 and older receive a 15% discount on most Amtrak fares. You can save sightseeing dollars if you are 62 or over by picking up a **Golden Age Passport** from any federally operated park, recreation area, historic site, wildlife refuge, or monument. There is a one-time fee of $10 that entitles holders to free admission to parks and other federally managed fee areas plus a 50% savings on camping fees.

Membership in the **American Association of Retired Persons (AARP),** 601 E St. NW, Washington, DC 20049 (☎ **800/424-3410** or 202/434-2277), entitles those 50 and older to discounts at numerous hotels, for rental cars, and at a few restaurants and attractions. The nonprofit **Elderhostel,** 75 Federal St., 3rd Floor, Boston, MA 02110 (☎ **617/ 426-7788;** www.elderhostel.org), has a great variety of inexpensive and interesting study programs, including room and board, for travelers ages 55 and older.

FOR STUDENTS

For inexpensive accommodations, as well as the opportunity to meet other traveling students, join **Hostelling International–American Youth Hostels,** Box 37613, Washington, DC 20013-7613 (☎ **202/783-6161;** fax 202/783-6171; www.hiayh.org; e-mail: hiayhserv@hiayh.org); for $3, or free with membership, they'll send a directory of all U.S. hostels. Twelve-month membership is free for those under 18, costs $25 for those ages 18 to 54, and is $15 for those 55 and older.

One of the best sources for information and bookings of discounted airfares, rail fares, and lodgings is the **Council on International Educational Exchange (CIEE),** 205 E. 42nd St., New York, NY 10017 (☎ **800/2-COUNCIL** or 212/822-2600; www.counciltravel.com), with offices throughout the United States.

5 Getting There

BY PLANE

Houston has two major airports: the George Bush Intercontinental Airport (IAH), and the smaller domestic William P. Hobby Airport.

GEORGE BUSH INTERCONTINENTAL AIRPORT (IAH)   As Houston's primary airport, Bush Intercontinental (☎ **281/233-1730;** www.ci.houston.tx.us/has/iah.html) is serviced by most major domestic carriers and functions as a hub for **Continental Airlines** (☎ 800/523-3273; www.flycontinental.com). Other domestic carriers include **America West** (☎ 800/235-9292; www.americawest.com), **American** (☎ 800/433-7300; www.aa.com), **Delta** (☎ 800/221-1212; www.delta.com), **Northwest** (☎ 800/225-2525; www.nwa.com), **Southwest** (☎ 800/435-9792; www.iflyswa.com), **TWA** (☎ 800/221-2000, www.twa.com), **United** (☎ 800/241-6522; www.ual.com), and **US Airways** (☎ 800/428-4322; www.usairways.com). Major international carriers servicing IAH include **AeroMexico** (☎ 800/237-6639; www.aeromexico.com), **Air Canada** (☎ 888/776-3000; www.aircanada.ca), **Air France** (☎ 800/237-2747; www.airfrance.com), **British Airways** (☎ 800/247-9297; www.british-airways.com), **KLM** (☎ 800/374-7747; www.klm.com), and **Lufthansa** (☎ 800/654-3880; www.lufthansa.com).

The "Drive Friendly" State

For years, the Texas Department of Transportation has been urging motorists to "drive friendly," and apparently many of them, especially in rural areas, have taken that message to heart. When you approach a vehicle from behind on a two-lane road more often than not that vehicle will pull onto the shoulder, while maintaining speed, to let you pass without having to go into the oncoming lane. Fortunately, most Texas state highways have good, wide shoulders so there's little danger. We're not sure if this is technically legal or not, but everybody in rural Texas does it, including state troopers.

WILLIAM P. HOBBY AIRPORT   Houston's Hobby Airport (www.ci.houston.tx.us/has/hou.html) is used mostly by **Southwest Airlines** (☎ 800/435-9792; www.iflyswa.com). Flights arrive from and depart to most areas in the contiguous United States.

BY CAR

Houston is connected to Dallas and Fort Worth by I-45; to San Antonio, New Orleans, and Beaumont by I-10. From Austin, you can take either Tex. 71 through Bastrop to Columbus, where it joins I-10, or you can take Tex. 290 east through Brenham.

If you aren't already a member, it's a good idea to join the **American Automobile Association (AAA)** (☎ 800/ 336-4357), which has hundreds of offices nationwide. AAA headquarters is at 3000 Southwest Freeway, Houston, TX 77098 (☎ 800/765-0766; www.aaa.com). Members can get excellent maps, tour guides, and emergency road service; they'll also help you plan an exact itinerary.

DRIVING RULES   Texas law requires all drivers to carry proof of insurance, as well as a valid driver's license. Safety belts are required in cars and light trucks for drivers and all front-seat passengers; children under age 4, regardless of where they're seated, must wear safety belts or be in approved child seats, and infants under 2 must be secured in car seats. The speed limits in Texas are more realistic than in surrounding states such as New Mexico. The maximum speed limit on interstate highways is 70 miles per hour; and the maximum on numbered noninterstates is 70 miles per hour during daylight and 65 miles per hour at night, unless otherwise posted. Motorcyclists are required to wear helmets, and radar detectors are permitted.

MAPS   A good state highway map can be obtained from the **Texas Department of Transportation,** Travel Division, 150 E. Riverside Dr., Austin, TX 78704 (☎ **800/888-8TEX;** www.traveltex.com). Otherwise, maps can be purchased at bookstores, gas stations, and most supermarkets and discount stores.

INSURANCE   Be sure to carry proof of automobile liability insurance, and be certain that your policy includes protection from uninsured motorists. If you're renting a car, check your credit cards to see if any of them include a collision-damage waiver (CDW) when you rent with their card; it can save you on the cost of your rental.

ROAD CONDITIONS   Texas roads are among the best in the western United States, and the state's generally moderate weather keeps snow closures to a minimum. However, hurricanes can cause flooding in late summer and early fall along the Gulf Coast. A recorded **24-hour hot line** (☎ **800/ 452-9292**) provides information on road conditions statewide, and information is also available online at **www.dot.state.tx.us/hcr/main.htm**.

ROADSIDE ASSISTANCE   In case of an accident or road emergency, contact the state police (☎ **911**), or, if that doesn't work dial "0" (zero) for the operator. American Automobile Association members can get free emergency road service by calling **AAA's emergency number** (☎ **800/AAA-HELP**).

BY TRAIN

Amtrak (☎ **800/USA-RAIL;** www.amtrak.com) has two routes through Texas. The **Sunset Limited** has stops at Beaumont/Port Arthur, Houston, San Antonio, Del Rio, Sanderson, Alpine, and El Paso on its New Orleans to Los Angeles run; and the **Texas Eagle,** from Chicago, stops at Texarkana, Mineola, Marshall, Longview, Dallas, Fort Worth, Cleburne, McGregor, Taylor, Austin, San Marcos, and San Antonio, where you can connect with the Sunset Limited.

6   For Foreign Visitors

ENTRY REQUIREMENTS

Immigration laws are a hot political issue in the United States these days, and the following requirements may have changed somewhat by the time you plan your trip. Check at any U.S. embassy or consulate for current information and requirements. You can also plug into the **U.S. State Department**'s Internet site at **http://state.gov**.

VISAS   The U.S. State Department has a **Visa Waiver Pilot Program** allowing citizens of certain countries to enter the United States without a visa for stays of up to 90 days. At press time these included Andorra, Argentina, Australia, Austria, Belgium, Brunei, Denmark, Finland, France, Germany, Iceland, Ireland, Italy, Japan, Liechtenstein, Luxembourg, Monaco, the Netherlands, New Zealand, Norway, San Marino, Slovenia, Spain, Sweden, Switzerland, and the United Kingdom. Citizens of these countries need only a valid passport and a round-trip air or cruise ticket in their possession upon arrival. If they first enter the United States, they may also visit Mexico, Canada, Bermuda, and/or the Caribbean islands and return to the United States without a visa. Further information is available from any U.S. embassy or consulate. Canadian citizens may enter the United States without visas; they need only proof of residence.

Citizens of all other countries must have (1) a valid passport that expires at least 6 months later than the scheduled end of their visit to the United States, and (2) a tourist visa, which may be obtained without charge from any U.S. consulate.

Obtaining a Visa   To obtain a visa, the traveler must submit a completed application form (either in person or by mail) with a 1½-inch-square photo and must demonstrate binding ties to a residence abroad. Usually you can obtain a visa at once or within 24 hours, but it may take longer during the summer rush from June through August. If you cannot go in person, contact the nearest U.S. embassy or consulate for directions on applying by mail. Your travel agent or airline office may also be able to provide you with visa applications and instructions. The U.S. consulate or embassy that issues your visa will determine whether you will be issued a multiple- or single-entry visa and any restrictions regarding the length of your stay.

British subjects can obtain up-to-date passport and visa information by calling the **U.S. Embassy Visa Information Line** (☎ **0891/200-290**) or the **London Passport Office** (☎ **0990/210-410** for recorded information).

MEDICAL REQUIREMENTS

Unless you're arriving from an area known to be suffering from an epidemic (particularly cholera or yellow fever), inoculations or vaccinations are not required for entry into the United States. If you have a disease that requires treatment with narcotics or syringe-administered medications, carry a valid signed prescription from your physician to allay any suspicions that you may be smuggling narcotics (a serious offense that carries severe penalties in the United States).

For HIV-positive visitors, requirements for entering the United States are somewhat vague and change frequently. For up-to-the-minute information concerning HIV-positive travelers, contact the Centers for Disease Control's **National Center for HIV** (☎ **404/332-4559;** www.hivatis.org) or the **Gay Men's Health Crisis** (☎ **212/367-1000;** www.gmhc.org).

DRIVER'S LICENSES

Foreign driver's licenses are mostly recognized in the United States, although you may want to get an **International Driver's License** if your home license is not written in English.

CUSTOMS REQUIREMENTS

Every visitor over 21 years of age may bring in, free of duty, the following: (1) 1 liter of wine or hard liquor; (2) 200 cigarettes, 100 cigars (but not from Cuba), or 3 pounds of smoking tobacco; and (3) $100 worth of gifts. These exemptions are offered to travelers who spend at least 72 hours in the United States and who have not claimed them within the preceding 6 months. It is altogether forbidden to bring into the country foodstuffs (particularly fruit, cooked meats, and canned goods) and plants (vegetables, seeds, tropical plants, and the like). Foreign tourists may bring in or take out up to $10,000 in U.S. or foreign currency with no formalities; larger sums must be declared to U.S. Customs on entering or leaving, which includes filing form CM 4790. For more specific information regarding U.S. Customs, call your nearest U.S. embassy or consulate, or the U.S. Customs office at ☎ **202/ 927-1770** or online at **www.customs.ustreas.gov**.

MONEY

The U.S. monetary system has a decimal base: One American **dollar** ($1) = 100 **cents** (100¢). Dollar bills commonly come in $1 (a "buck"), $5, $10, $20, $50, and $100 denominations. The last two are not welcome when paying for small purchases and are usually not accepted in taxis or at subway ticket booths. Note that bills in most of the common denominations were recently redesigned, so you will likely see $100, $50, $10, and $5 notes in two different styles, both of which are legal tender.

There are six coin denominations: 1¢ (one cent or a "penny"); 5¢ (five cents or a "nickel"); 10¢ (ten cents or a "dime"); 25¢ (twenty-five cents or a "quarter"); 50¢ (fifty cents or a "half dollar"); and the $1 pieces (the large silver Eisenhower coin, the smaller Susan B. Anthony coin, and the new golden Sacagawea coin).

The "foreign-exchange bureaus" so common in Europe are rare even at airports in the United States, and nonexistent outside major cities. It's best not to change foreign money (or traveler's checks denominated in a currency other than U.S. dollars) at a small-town bank, or even a branch in a big city; in fact, leave any currency other than U.S. dollars at home (except the cash you need for the taxi or bus ride home when you return to your own country)—it may prove a greater nuisance to you than it's worth.

Traveler's checks in U.S. dollars are accepted at most hotels, motels, restaurants, and large stores. Sometimes picture identification is required. Visa, American Express, and Thomas Cook traveler's checks are readily accepted in the United States. Be sure to record the numbers of the checks, and keep that information separate in case they get lost or stolen.

Credit cards are the method of payment most widely used: Visa (BarclayCard in Britain), MasterCard (Eurocard in Europe, Access in Britain, Diamond in Japan), American Express, Discover, Diners Club, enRoute, Japan Credit Bank, and Carte Blanche, in descending order of acceptance. You can save yourself trouble by using "plastic" rather than cash or traveler's checks in 95% of all hotels, motels, restaurants, and retail stores. A credit card can also serve as a deposit for renting a car, as proof of identity, or as a "cash card," enabling you to draw money from automated teller machines (ATMs) that accept them. Expect to be charged up to $3 per transaction, however, if you're not using your own bank's ATM. One way around these fees is to ask for cash back at grocery stores that accept ATM cards and don't charge usage fees. Of course, you'll have to purchase something first.

If you plan to travel for several weeks or more in the United States, you may want to deposit enough money into your credit-card account to cover anticipated expenses and avoid finance charges in your absence. This also reduces the likelihood of your receiving an unwelcome big bill on your return.

You can telegraph money, or have it telegraphed to you very quickly, using the **Western Union** system (☎ **800/ 325-6000**).

INSURANCE

Although it's not required of travelers, health insurance is highly recommended. Unlike many European countries, the United States does not usually offer free or low-cost medical care to its citizens or visitors. Doctors and hospitals are expensive, and in most cases will require advance payment or proof of coverage before they render their services. Though lack of health insurance may prevent you from being admitted to a hospital in non-emergencies, don't worry about being left on a street corner to die: The American way is to fix you now and bill the living daylights out of you later.

Insurance policies can cover everything from the loss or theft of your baggage and trip cancellation to the guarantee of bail in case you're arrested. Good policies will also cover the costs of an accident, repatriation, or death. See "Health & Insurance" in earlier in this chapter for more information. Packages such as **Europ Assistance** in Europe are sold by automobile clubs and travel agencies at attractive rates. **Worldwide Assistance Services, Inc.** (☎ **800/821-2828**) is the agent for Europ Assistance in the United States.

SAFETY

While tourist areas are generally safe, crime is on the increase in many areas, and urban centers in the United States tend to be less safe than those in Europe or Japan. Visitors should always stay alert. This is particularly true of large U.S. cities such as Houston and Dallas. It's wise to ask the city's or area's tourist office if you're in doubt about which neighborhoods are unsafe.

Remember also that hotels are open to the public, and in a large hotel, security may not be able to screen everyone entering. Always lock your room door—don't assume that once inside your hotel you are automatically safe and no longer need be aware of your surroundings.

DRIVING   Safety while driving is particularly important. Question your rental agency about personal safety and ask for a traveler-safety brochure when you pick up your car. Obtain written directions—or a map with the route clearly marked— from the agency showing how to get to your destination. (Many agencies now offer the option of renting a cellular phone for the duration of your car rental; check with the rental agent when you pick up the car.) And, if possible, arrive and depart during daylight hours.

Recently, more and more crime has involved cars and drivers. If you drive off a highway into a dubious neighborhood, leave the area as quickly as possible. If you have an accident, even on the highway, stay in your car with the doors locked until you assess the situation or until the police arrive. If you're bumped from behind on the street or are involved in a minor accident with no injuries and the situation appears to be suspicious, motion to the other driver to follow you. Never get out of your car in such situations. Go directly to the nearest police precinct, well-lit service station, or 24-hour store.

Always try to park in well-lit and well-traveled areas if possible. You're probably safer leaving your rental car unlocked and empty of your valuables than if you lock your car with valuables in plain view. Never leave any packages or valuables in sight. If someone attempts to rob you or steal your car, don't try to resist the thief/carjacker—report the incident to the police department immediately by calling ☎ **911.**

FAST FACTS: For the Foreign Traveler

Electricity   The United States uses 110–120 volts AC (60 cycles), as compared to 220–240 volts AC (50 cycles) used in most of Europe, Australia, and New Zealand. In addition to a

100-volt converter, small appliances of non-American manu-
facture, such as hair dryers or shavers, will require a plug
adapter, with two flat, parallel pins. Downward converters that
change 220–240 volts to 110–120 volts are difficult to find in
the United States, so bring one with you.

Embassies/Consulates   All embassies are located in the
nation's capital, Washington, D.C.; some consulates are located
in major cities, and most nations have a mission to the United
Nations in New York City. Call directory information in
Washington, D.C. (☎ **202/555-1212**) for the phone number
of your national embassy.

The following countries have consulates in Texas: **Belgium,**
2929 Allen Parkway, Houston (☎ 713/529-0775); **Britain,**
2911 Turtle Creek Blvd., Dallas (☎ 214/521-4090) and 1000
Louisiana St., Houston (☎ 713/659-6270); **Canada,** 750 N.
Saint Paul St., Dallas (☎ 214/922-9806); **Costa Rica,** 6836
San Pedro Ave., San Antonio (☎ 210/824-8474); **El Sal-
vador,** 1555 W. Mockingbird Lane, Dallas (☎ 214/
637-1018); **Germany,** 1330 Post Oak Blvd., Houston
(☎ 713/627-7770); **Haiti,** 6310 Auden St., Houston (☎ 713/
661-8275); **Israel,** 1 E. Greenway Plaza, Houston (☎ 713/
627-3780); **Italy,** 6255 W. Northwest Highway, Apt. 304,
Dallas (☎ 214/368-4113); **Malta,** 500 N. Akard St., Dallas
(☎ 214/855-9897); **Mexico,** 910 E. San Antonio Ave., El
Paso (☎ 915/533-3645), 8855 N. Stemmons Freeway, Dallas
(☎ 214/630-7341), 511 W. Ohio Ave., Midland (☎ 915/
687-2334), 724 E. Elizabeth St., Brownsville (☎ 956/
542-4431), 600 S. Broadway St., McAllen (☎ 956/630-1777),
and 200 E. 6th St., Austin (☎ 512/478-2866); **Nicaragua,**
2825 Wilcrest Dr., Houston (☎ 713/953-0237); **Norway,**
2777 Allen Parkway, Houston (☎ 713/521-2900); and
Qatar, 1990 Post Oak Blvd., Houston (☎ 713/355-8221).

Gasoline (Petrol)   Petrol is known as gasoline (or simply
"gas") in the United States, and petrol stations are known as
both gas stations and service stations—an odd name since
almost all the service stations you'll encounter in Texas are self-
serve. One U.S. gallon equals 3.75 liters, while 1.2 U.S. gallons
equals 1 Imperial gallon. You'll notice there are several grades
(and price levels) of gasoline available at most gas stations, and
that their names change from company to company. Unleaded
gasoline with the highest octane is the most expensive, but

most rental cars will run fine with the less expensive "regular" unleaded. Texas often has among the lowest gasoline prices in the United States, and although prices fluctuate, at press time the regular unleaded gas cost in Texas ranged from $1.30 to $1.55 per gallon, with the lowest prices in the Gulf Coast area.

Holidays   Banks, government offices, post offices, and many stores, restaurants, and museums are closed on the following legal national holidays: January 1 (New Year's Day), the third Monday in January (Martin Luther King Jr. Day), the third Monday in February (Presidents' Day, Washington's Birthday), the last Monday in May (Memorial Day), July 4 (Independence Day), the first Monday in September (Labor Day), the second Monday in October (Columbus Day), November 11 (Veterans' Day/Armistice Day), the fourth Thursday in November (Thanksgiving Day), and December 25 (Christmas). Also, the Tuesday following the first Monday in November is Election Day and is a federal government holiday in presidential-election years (held every 4 years, and next in 2004).

Legal Aid   The foreign tourist will probably never become involved with the American legal system. If you are "pulled over" for a minor infraction (for example, of the highway code, such as speeding), never attempt to pay the fine directly to a police officer; this could be construed as attempted bribery, a much more serious crime. Pay fines by mail, or directly into the hands of the clerk of the court. If accused of a more serious offense, say and do nothing before consulting a lawyer. Here, the burden is on the state to prove a person's guilt beyond a reasonable doubt, and everyone has the right to remain silent, whether he or she is suspected of a crime or actually arrested. Once arrested, a person can make one telephone call to a party of his or her choice. Call your embassy or consulate (see above).

Mail   If you want your mail to follow you on your vacation and you aren't sure of your address, your mail can be sent to you, in your name, c/o General Delivery at the main post office of the city or region where you expect to be (call ☎ **800/275-8777** or check www.usps.gov on the Internet for information on the nearest post office). The addressee must pick mail up in person and must produce proof of identity (driver's license or passport). Most post offices will hold your mail for up to 1 month. Post offices in cities are usually open Monday to Friday from 8am to 6pm, and Saturday from 9am to 3pm. Those in smaller towns will usually have shorter hours.

Mailboxes are blue with a blue-and-white eagle logo, and carry the inscription UNITED STATES POSTAL SERVICE. If your mail is addressed to a U.S. destination, don't forget to add the five-digit postal code, or ZIP (zone improvement plan) code, after the two-letter abbreviation of the state to which the mail is addressed.

Within the United States, at press time, it cost 20¢ to mail a standard-size postcard and 34¢ for a letter. An international airmail letter of up to ½ ounce costs 80¢ (60¢ to Canada and Mexico), and an international postcard costs 70¢ (50¢ to Canada and Mexico). A preprinted postal aerogramme costs 70¢.

Taxes   In the United States, there is no VAT (value-added tax) or other indirect tax at a national level. Every state, as well as each city and county, has the right to levy its own local tax on all purchases, including hotel and restaurant checks, airline tickets, and so on. Sales tax is almost never included in the price tags you'll see on merchandise or in the rates you're quoted for lodging. These taxes are nonrefundable.

Tipping   Tipping is so ingrained in the American way of life that the annual income tax of tip-earning service personnel is based on how much they should have received in light of their employers' gross revenues. Accordingly, they may have to pay tax on a tip you didn't actually give them.

Suggestions for tipping include: **bartenders** 10% to 15%; **bellhops** $1 per bag ($2 to $3 if you have a lot of luggage); **cab drivers** 15% of the fare; **chamber staff** $1 per day; **checkroom attendants** $1 per garment; **restaurant service staff** 15% to 20% of the check; and **valet parking attendants** $1. Tipping is not expected at gas stations and fast-food restaurants.

3

Getting to Know Houston

This chapter provides an overview of the Houston metropolitan area, with plenty of advice on how to navigate your way through its sprawl. You'll also find a list of useful resources, from weather information to hospital and drugstore locations.

1 Orientation

ARRIVING

BY PLANE

Houston's primary airport, the **George Bush Intercontinental Airport** (IAH), is located 22 miles north of downtown, and the smaller, domestic **William P. Hobby Airport** is located 9 miles southeast of downtown.

GETTING TO & FROM IAH   **Taxi** service from IAH to downtown costs about $42 and the ride takes 40 minutes; getting to the Galleria-area hotel district costs a few dollars more.

Express Shuttle USA (☎ 713/523-8000) ferries passengers from the airport to the major hotels downtown, the Galleria area, the Medical Center, and the Greenway Plaza. Service is from 7:30am to 11:30pm. The 40-minute ride to or from downtown costs $19 ($34 round-trip) per person; one-way and round-trip fares for the other three locations are $20 and $36. Shuttle buses collect passengers within 15 minutes of a requested pick-up. Shuttle ticket counters are at each of the airport terminals.

Another option is the **city's bus service** (☎ 713/635-4000), which operates Monday through Friday only from 6:30am to 7pm between Terminal C and downtown. The fare is either $1 or $1.50, depending on the time; exact change is required. Buses run every 30 minutes, and travel time to downtown is a little less than an hour.

All of the major **car-rental** companies are represented at each of the terminals. John F. Kennedy Boulevard is the main artery into the airport. When leaving the airport, you'll see signs pointing the way toward the North Freeway (I-45) to the right and toward the Eastex Freeway (Tex. 59) to the left. Take the Eastex, which is shorter and generally quicker for most parts of town.

GETTING TO & FROM HOBBY AIRPORT All the major **car-rental** agencies have counters here with either staff or a service phone.

Taxis from Hobby to the downtown area cost about $30, and to the Galleria area $40.

Express Shuttle USA buses (☎ **713/523-8000**) cost about $15 to downtown, the Galleria area, the Medical Center, and Greenway Plaza, and can take passengers to Houston Intercontinental for $20. Operating hours are the same as for the Houston Intercontinental Airport, except for the shuttle service between the airports, which stops at 9pm.

BY TRAIN

Amtrak (☎ **800/872-7245;** www.amtrak.com) trains from New Orleans, Chicago, and Los Angeles (and points in between) arrive and depart from the **Southern Pacific Station** at 902 Washington Ave. (☎ **713/224-1577**), close to downtown.

VISITOR INFORMATION

The **Greater Houston Convention and Visitor's Bureau** has a shiny new visitor center located in the City Hall Building at 901 Bagby St. between Walker and McKinney (☎ **713/ 227-3100**). Here you can get brochures for just about anything, a range of city maps, architectural and historical guides, and answers from the helpful staff. You can also play with the interactive computer stations, see a short introductory film of the city, and find out about what events will be occurring during your stay. The center is open daily from 9am to 4pm, and can be reached by foot from any downtown hotel. If you're driving, you'll need to park your car at the underground lot that is one block north of city hall. To get there, turn onto Walker, drive past City Hall, and immediately turn right on Bagby, then right again on Rusk; you'll see a sign that says THEATER DISTRICT PARKING 2. It's free for visitors; just get your parking ticket stamped at the visitor center.

CITY LAYOUT

Houston is a difficult city to know in depth; it was built with no master plan, and most of its streets are jumbled together with little continuity. To complicate matters, the suburban areas look a lot alike and have street names that sound similar, and because the terrain is so flat, the only visible points of reference are tall buildings. Salespersons, repair persons, and others who have to travel about the city rely on something called a "Key Map"—a binder of detailed maps that divides Houston into a grid system with each square in the grid having its own map. This homegrown Houston creation became so popular here that it was copied by map companies in other cities, though it may offer more information than many visitors want. Standard street maps can be found at any drugstore and many convenience stores, and some helpful maps of downtown, the Museum District, and the broad outlines of the city can be obtained from the visitors center in City Hall. But most of the main attractions that visitors will want to see are not far off the freeways and other main arteries; with a basic knowledge of these, you can keep your bearings in Houston pretty well as long as you don't stray too far off the beaten path.

To understand the basic layout of Houston's freeways, it's best to picture an irregularly shaped spider web. The lines that radiate out from the center are in the following clockwise order: At 1 o'clock is the **Eastex Freeway** (Tex. 59 north), which usually has signs saying CLEVELAND, a town in east Texas; at 3 o'clock is the **East Freeway** (I-10 east to Beaumont and New Orleans); between 4 and 5 o'clock is the **Gulf Freeway** (I-45 south to Galveston); at 6 o'clock is the **South Freeway** (Tex. 228 to Lake Jackson and Freeport); between 7 and 8 o'clock is the **Southwest Freeway** (Tex. 59 to Laredo, look for signs that read VICTORIA); at 9 o'clock is the **Katy Freeway** (I-10 west to San Antonio); at 10 o'clock is the **Northwest Freeway** (Tex. 290 to Austin); and at 11 o'clock is the **North Freeway** (I-45 north to Dallas). As the freeways approach the downtown area, they form a tight loop that has actually come to define the geographical borders of downtown. Also, there are two circular freeways that connect these highways to each other in the same manner as the concentric circular strands of a spider web. The first is **Loop 610** (known as "the Loop"), which has a 4- to 5-mile radius from downtown. The second is known alternately as **Sam Houston Parkway** or Beltway 8. It has a 10- to 15-mile radius from downtown and is mostly a toll road except for the section near the Bush Intercontinental Airport.

In addition to the freeways, there are certain arteries in the most visited parts of town—the western and southwestern parts of the city—that most newcomers would do well to know. (The attractions in the southeast can be located using the Gulf Freeway as a reference.) Here, then, are brief descriptions of the main thoroughfares:

Main Street, which heads south-southwest from the city's center, intersects Montrose Boulevard a couple of miles from downtown at a traffic circle called the Mecom Fountain; this is the heart of the Museum District. Beyond the fountain, Main Street passes Hermann Park, the Texas Medical Center, and the Rice University campus. This stretch of South Main is lined with beautiful oak trees, which were planted in remembrance of the Texans who died in World War I. After the Medical Center, South Main passes close by the Astrodome.

From the Mecom Fountain, where it intersects South Main Street, **Montrose Boulevard** runs due north, crosses West-heimer Road and then meets Buffalo Bayou. It gives its name to the Montrose area (see "Neighborhoods in Brief," below) and is lined by several bistros around the Museum District. After it crosses the bayou, Montrose Boulevard becomes Studemont and then Studewood when it enters a historic neighborhood known as the Heights.

Westheimer Road is the east-west axis around which most of western Houston turns. It begins in the Montrose area and continues for many miles through various urban and suburban landscapes without ever seeming to come to an end. Past the Montrose area, Westheimer crosses Kirby Drive. To your right will be River Oaks, home to Houston's wealthy residents. Farther along are Highland Village Shopping Center, Loop 610, and the Galleria/Post Oak district, also known as Uptown. Beyond Uptown, Westheimer is decorated with fast-food restaurants, gasoline stations, and chain retail stores as it continues through suburbia.

Another important artery is **Kirby Drive.** From where it intersects Westheimer Road by River Oaks, it continues due south skirting the Greenway Plaza (see "Neighborhoods in Brief," below) and passing under the Southwest Freeway. South of the freeway Kirby enters University Place, which stretches around the Rice University campus and is the favorite residential area for Houston's doctors, lawyers, and other professionals. Kirby eventually intersects South Main Street in the vicinity of the Astrodome.

NEIGHBORHOODS IN BRIEF

Downtown   Once a ghost town in the evenings and week-ends, downtown Houston is now the place to be. Restaurants and bars are opening (and in some cases closing) in quick suc-cession; hotels are enjoying boom times, and several new hotels are in various stages of planning and construction. Much of the revitalization is taking place on the northwest side of downtown, in and around Old Market Square and the theater district, where Houston's symphony orchestra, ballet, opera, and its principal theater company all reside. To the east, within walking distance, are the George Brown Convention Center and the new baseball park, Enron Field.

A network of tunnels and elevated walkways that total more than six miles connects most of downtown. Shops and restau-rants line these tunnels, forming a sort of underground city. As is typical of Houston, almost all of these pedestrian tunnels are private developments and not public projects. South of downtown is midtown, an area in transition, with townhouses and shops gradually replacing vacant lots and small office buildings. Vietnamese shopkeepers and restaurateurs have set-tled into the western side (look for street signs in Vietnamese), especially along Milam Street, where you can find an array of excellent Vietnamese restaurants with reasonable prices.

East End   Before Houston was established on the banks of Buffalo Bayou, the town of Harrisburg already existed two miles downstream. As Houston grew eastward, it incorporated Harrisburg, leaving behind little of the old town. The inner East End is an up-and-coming neighborhood of mixed eth-nicity. There is a small commercial Chinatown a couple of blocks east of the convention center; beyond that, the area becomes residential, eventually mixing with small-scale manufacturing, auto mechanic and body shops, and service industries for the ship channel. Continuing farther out is NASA's Space Center Houston; Kemah, which is something like Houston's version of Fisherman's Wharf; and Galveston Island. Most of the hotels located in this area are along the Gulf Freeway. The main reason for staying here is that the hotel rates are, for the most part, moderate, and the location between downtown, Hobby Airport, and the abovementioned attractions makes the East End convenient.

South Main   South of downtown and midtown is the Museum District and Hermann Park. This is a lovely part of town with lots of green space, and most of the museums are set within a few blocks of each other. Here also are the Houston Zoological Gardens and the Rice University campus, and south of the park begins the highly regarded Texas Medical Center. Beyond that is the Astrodome area, with AstroWorld and WaterWorld, an exhibition hall and a new football stadium in construction—all of which is now called Reliant Park. There are many hotels on South Main to suit all budgets. This is a also a convenient location for trips to downtown, to Uptown, or to the Kirby District of restaurants and shops.

Montrose   Directly west of downtown is this hip, artsy, and colorful part of town known for its clubs, galleries, and shops. The Museum District extends into the southern part of Montrose to include the famous Menil Collection and its satellite galleries, which are a must-see for any visitor interested in the arts. Upscale in certain sections, downscale in others, Montrose contains a broad cross-section of Houston society. It is also the de facto center of Houston's large and active gay community. With downtown to the east, the South Main area to the south, the Kirby District to the west (with Uptown just beyond that), and the Heights to the north, it is nothing if not centrally located. What's more, it has some of the best restaurants in the city.

Kirby District & Greenway Plaza   The area bordering Kirby Drive from River Oaks to University Place offers the most restaurants of any other district in Houston; it's great hunting ground for adventurous diners. Near Kirby Drive's midway point, where it crosses the Southwest Freeway, is the

Greenway Plaza, an integrated development of office buildings, movie theaters, a sports arena, and shops. Farther south is the Rice Village, a retail development consisting of 16 square blocks of smart shops and restaurants. It is phenomenally popular with Houstonians and visitors, and attracts all kinds of shoppers and diners.

Uptown (Galleria/Post Oak) Farther west, all the way to the Loop 610, is where Uptown begins. It is still informally called the Galleria area, after the large indoor shopping mall, entertainment, and hotel complex. But, the district's business owners had to devise another name for it because the developer of the Galleria protected the use of its name so jealously (and so effectively with his battery of corporate lawyers) that it became problematic to use the word in any commercial context. Thus, we have "Uptown." This area has the greatest concentration of hotels in the city. Aside from the Galleria, most of the shopping malls and stores front Post Oak Boulevard from Westheimer Road north for a half-mile to a mall called Uptown Park. You'll know you're in Uptown when you see the futuristic traffic lights, arches, and street signs at the intersections.

The Heights & North Houston All the neighborhoods described above are south of I-10, which cuts Houston into northern and southern halves. North Houston is largely a mix of working- and middle-class neighborhoods and commercial centers and, with the exception of the Heights, has little to offer visitors. Over the years, developers tried to establish upscale communities here, but an inherent quality of suburbanism is that you can always build farther out, and, with each successive subdivision, the inner suburbs lose a little more of their luster. Ultimately, the developers took this to its logical extreme, skipping over vast tracts of land to build so far north that the city will never touch them. Thus, we have The Woodlands and Kingwood, two upscale residential developments so far out that one has difficulty considering them as part of Houston.

The Heights, interestingly enough, could have served as the original model for the subdivisions that came later; it was conceived as an independent, planned residential community in the 1890s and remained so until 1918 when it was annexed by

Houston. Many of the houses one finds in the area are lovely, turn-of-the-century, Texas Victorians. The Heights is a peaceful neighborhood close to downtown and the Montrose area, but note: The Heights is "dry" (the sale of alcohol is forbidden) and, as a consequence, there are no good restaurants here.

2 Getting Around

BY CAR

Houston is organized around the personal automobile. A car is almost a necessity unless you confine your explorations largely to the downtown area and the Museum District. Buses linking these two areas are frequent and easy to use so that it's possible to stay in a downtown or South Main hotel and get around by bus, the hotel shuttle (if available), and, perhaps, the occasional taxi. Otherwise, you'll probably need a car. Traffic can be a problem, however, and Houston's freeways are no place for the meek: Many drivers don't obey speed limits, bob and weave through the lanes, and make their turnoffs at the last possible moment. The best thing to do is make sure you have a clear idea of where you're headed and what exit you'll need to take before you get on the freeway. As freeway systems go, however, Houston's is logical and has good directional signs. Traffic in Houston can be heavy throughout the day, especially during rush hour or when there's freeway construction. You can use the **Texas Department of Transportation Info Hotline** number (☎ 713/802-5074) to check for lane closures on local freeways. The *Houston Chronicle* also provides this information.

RENTALS   The prices for rental cars in Houston are generally lower than those for many tourist destinations, but there is a large tax that raises the price by 27%. Keep this in mind when making your budget and when the sales person tries to bump you up to a higher-priced model. As is the case when renting cars anywhere, you probably don't need to buy extra insurance if you're already covered by your personal auto insurance or the credit card you're paying with. The major rental car companies with locations around the city include: **Alamo** (☎ 800/327-9633), **Avis** (☎ 800/831-2847), **Budget** (☎ 800/527-7000), **Dollar** (☎ 800/800-4000), **Enterprise** (☎ 800/736-8222), **Hertz** (☎ 800/654-3131),

National (☎ 800/227-7368), and **Thrifty** (☎ 800/847-4389).

BY PUBLIC TRANSPORTATION

The **Metropolitan Transportation Authority** (MTA) (☎ **713/635-4000** or www.ridemetro.org) operates citywide bus service with stops indicated by red, white, or blue signs. Customer service staff can tell you what bus to take (and where to pick it up) to any specific destination you give them. There are five free Metro Trolley routes that circle through the downtown area and are quite handy for visitors. You can pick up a map of these routes at the **Houston Visitors Center** in City Hall (see "Visitor Information" earlier in this chapter). The standard fare is $1; for express buses it's $1.50 (seniors pay 40¢ and children under 4 ride free); exact change is required, and the machines accept dollar bills. On average, buses run every 30 minutes but become less frequent in the late hours of the evening.

BY TAXI

Taxis are plentiful in the city, but trying to hail one on the street can be an exercise in frustration. Call ahead or use hotel taxi stands. The principal companies are **Yellow Cab** (☎ 713/236-1111), **Fiesta Cab** (☎ 713/225-2666), **Liberty Cab** (☎ 713/695-6700), and **United Cab** (☎ 713/699-0000). Rates are set by the city: $3 for the first mile; $1.50 for each additional mile.

FAST FACTS: Houston

American Express   There is an office at 5085 Westheimer, Suite 4600, on the third floor of the Galleria Mall II (☎ **713/626-5740**). It's open Monday through Friday from 9am to 6pm and Saturday from 10am to 5pm.

Area Codes   Houston has 10-digit dialing for local calls. All numbers must begin with either of Houston's two area codes, 713 or 281.

Airports   See "Arriving," earlier in this chapter.

Car Rentals   See "Getting Around," earlier in this chapter.

Dentist   For a referral, call ☎ **800/922-6588** or 281/416-0692.

Doctor   For minor emergencies or to see a doctor without an appointment, call **Texas Urgent Care** at ☎ **800/417-2347.**

Drugstores   **Walgreens,** 3317 Montrose Blvd. at Hawthorne Street (☎ **713/520-7777**), is open 24 hours a day. In the vicinity of the Medical Center, there is a 24-hour **Eckerd Drug Store** at 7900 South Main St. (☎ **713/660-8934**).

Emergencies   In a police, fire, or medical emergency, call ☎ **911.**

Hospitals   The **Ben Taub General Hospital,** 1502 Taub Loop near the Texas Medical Center (☎ **713/793-2000**), is a nationally recognized emergency center.

Internet Access   Copy.com, 1201-F Westheimer in the Montrose area (☎ **713/528-1201**), has several computers, and is open from 9am to midnight on weekdays, 9am to 8pm on weekends.

Maps   See "City Layout," earlier in this chapter.

Newspapers & Magazines   The local, daily newspaper is the *Houston Chronicle.* The *Houston Press,* a weekly freebie that covers local politics and culture, can be found around town at restaurants, stores and just about anywhere people congregate.

Police   Dial ☎ **911.**

Post Office   The downtown branch, 401 Franklin St. (☎ **713/226-3066**), is open Monday through Friday from 9am to 5pm and Saturday from 9am to noon.

Safety   Exercise caution at night in the downtown areas that lie outside the theater district. See "Safety" in chapter 2.

Taxes   The local hotel tax is 17%; the local sales tax 8.25%.

Taxis   See "Getting Around," earlier in this chapter.

Transit Information   Call ☎ **713/802-5074.**

Weather   Call ☎ **713/529-4444.**

4

Accommodations

*T*hese days the hotel industry in Houston is in a curious state
of affairs. In the downtown area, which has become immensely
popular in the last few years, there are only four hotels, while
along several freeways, all the way to the edge of the city, you
will find major hotels (always with large conference facilities)
offering a full array of amenities. These hotels want it both
ways: They like the relatively cheap real estate, and they claim
that they are conveniently located to downtown, the Galleria
area, and the major attractions (with estimated driving times
that are possible only in the dead of night). While these hotels
are a great option for business people who are attending conferences within them or who have business in nearby office
parks, they are not the best choice for travelers who want to
explore Houston. On the other hand, Uptown has the greatest concentration of hotels in the city, and its popularity with
visitors never seems to wane. Certainly, the area's many
options makes it an exciting place to be, but don't make
Uptown your automatic choice without first giving some
thought to where you'll be spending your time in Houston.
See the "Neighborhoods in Brief" section in chapter 3 for
more suggestions about where to stay. The hotel listings that
follow include "rack rates" (the base retail price for a room
with no discount) for double occupancy with either two full-
size beds or one king-size bed, unless otherwise noted, as is
often the case with B&Bs. You should use this as a basis for
comparison and not think of these prices as etched in stone.
Always ask about discounts and special rates when making
reservations, particularly at large chain hotels. Keep in mind
that Houston has a hefty 17% hotel tax, which is not included
in the rates shown here and is rarely included in hotel price
quotes. Expect lodgings, particularly in the "Very Expensive"
and "Expensive" categories, to have such in-room amenities as
hair dryers, irons, and coffeemakers, unless otherwise noted.

Central Houston Accommodations

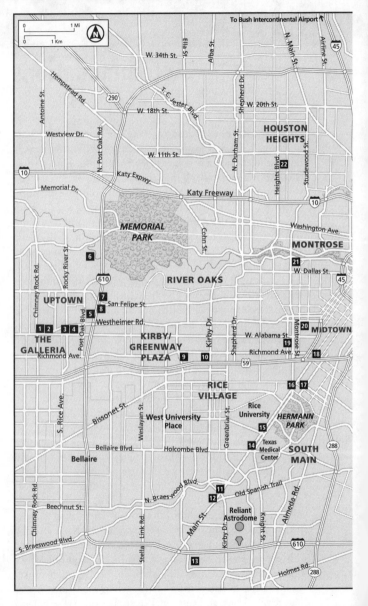

To Bush Intercontinental Airport

W. 34th St.
Ella St.
Alba St.
N. Main St.
Airline St.
45

Hempstead Rd.
290
T. C. Jester Blvd.
Shepherd Dr.
W. 20th St.
W. 18th St.

Antoine St.
Westview Dr.
N. Post Oak Rd.
W. 11th St.
N. Durham St.
HOUSTON HEIGHTS

Heights Blvd.
Studewood St.
22

10
Katy Expwy.
Memorial Dr.
Katy Freeway
10

MEMORIAL PARK
Cohn St.
Washington Ave.
MONTROSE
21
W. Dallas St.
45

6
610
RIVER OAKS

UPTOWN
Chimney Rock Rd.
Rocky River St.
7 San Felipe St.
8
5
Westheimer Rd.

1 2 3 4
Post Oak Blvd.
THE GALLERIA
Richmond Ave.

KIRBY/ GREENWAY PLAZA
Kirby Dr.
Shepherd Dr.
W. Alabama St.
Montrose St.
20 MIDTOWN
19
Richmond Ave.
18
59
9 10

RICE VILLAGE

S. Rice Ave.
Bissonet St.
Weslayan St.
West University Place
Greenbriar St.
Rice University
16 17

15
HERMANN PARK
288

Bellaire Blvd.
Holcombe Blvd.
14 Texas Medical Center
SOUTH MAIN

Bellaire
Chimney Rock Rd.

Beechnut St.
N. Braeswood Blvd.
11 Old Spanish Trail
12
Reliant Astrodome
Kirby Dr.
Knight St.
Almeda Rd.

S. Braeswood Blvd.
Stella
Link Rd.
Main St.
13
610
Holmes Rd.
288

0   1 Mi
0   1 Km
N

Allen Park Inn **21**
Astrodome Medical Center Hotel **12**
Days Inn Downtown Medical Center **18**
Doubletree Allen Center **23**
Doubletree Club Houston Near Greenway **10**
Doubletree Guest Suites **1**
Drury Inn and Suites Near the Galleria **7**
Four Seasons Hotel Houston Center **26**
Grant Palm Court Inn **11**
Hilton Houston Plaza **15**
Hilton University of Houston **27**
Holiday Inn Hotel & Suites Houston
   Medical Center **14**
Hyatt Regency **25**
J.W. Marriott Hotel by the Galleria **2**

La Colombe d'Or **19**
La Quinta Inn–Astrodome **13**
La Quinta Inn & Suites Galleria Area **8**
Lancaster Hotel **24**
Lovett Inn **20**
Omni Houston Hotel **6**
Park Plaza Warwick **16**
Patrician Bed and Breakfast Inn **17**
Red Carpet Inn Hobby Regency
   Motor Lodge **28**
Renaissance Houston Hotel **9**
Sara's Bed and Breakfast Inn **22**
Sheraton Suites Houston Near the Galleria **5**
Westin Galleria **3**
Westin Oaks **4**

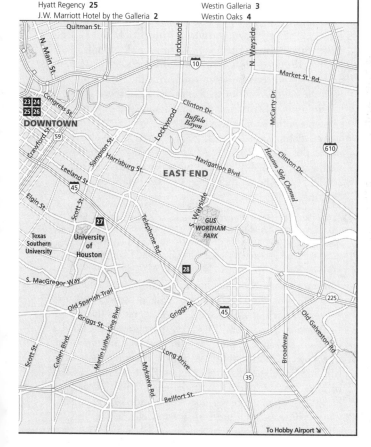

1 Downtown

VERY EXPENSIVE

Doubletree Allen Center. 400 Dallas, Houston, TX 77002. ☎ **800/ 222-TREE** or 713/759-0202. Fax 713/752-2734. www.doubletreehotels.com. 341 units. A/C TV TEL. $230 double. AE, DC, DISC, MC, V. Valet parking $17.

While staying here you won't feel like you're in a large hotel with 20 floors and more than 300 rooms; there's a coziness about it that the designers very cleverly captured. Rooms are midsize and furnished attractively in modern style with a bit more character than most hotel rooms. Bathrooms are large and well lit with plenty of counter space. The beds are comfortable, and each room includes a writing table and an armchair with ottoman. The hotel is situated in the middle of the business district, a block from the Hyatt Regency Houston. In amenities and service, it compares with the Hyatt, but not with the Four Seasons or the Lancaster (all reviewed below).

Dining: One restaurant for fine dining, one for informal dining, a coffee shop, and a lobby bar.

Amenities: A small fitness room, but guests can also make use of the downtown YMCA, which is actually a large, very well equipped facility about 6 blocks away. Services include concierge, 24-hour room service, same-day laundry/dry cleaning.

✪ **Four Seasons Hotel Houston Center.** 1300 Lamar St., Houston, TX 77010. ☎ **800/332-3442** or 713/650-1300. Fax 713/276-4787. www. fourseasons.com. 399 units. A/C MINIBAR TV TEL. $335–$385 double, $365–$900 suite. Children under 18 stay free in parents' room. Weekend rates and packages available. AE, CB, DC, ER, JCB, MC, V. Valet parking $18.

This member of the luxury hotel chain does everything right. It stands out especially in the areas of service (reliable concierge, very attentive staff, excellent restaurant, and a European spa) and spaciousness (everything about the hotel is large—guest rooms, suites, the gym, and all common areas). The hotel is located near the city's convention center and within easy walking distance of Enron Field, the new baseball park. Across the street from the hotel are The Park Shops, a downtown shopping center, and the Houston Center Athletic Club, whose facilities are available to Four Seasons' guests. Standard rooms come with one king-size bed or two twin beds, a large writing table, and an easy chair. Bathrooms are large and well equipped.

Dining/Diversions: Chef Tim Keating's cooking has made the **DeVille Restaurant** the favorite downtown spot for fine dining. The food is contemporary French, the ambience is formal, and the service is excellent. The more casual **Terrace Café** offers good food in a relaxed setting. There's also a poolside cafe open during the season, and the quiet lobby bar is perfect for unwinding after a grueling day.

Amenities: Spa, a very large and well-equipped gym, sauna, whirlpool, outdoor pool on fourth-floor terrace, access to facilities of Houston Center Athletic Club, complimentary Towncar for trips within downtown area, fax machine delivered to room on request, bathrobes, makeup mirror, 24-hour room service, concierge.

✪ **Lancaster Hotel.** 701 Texas Ave., Houston, TX 77002. ☎ **800/231-0336** or 713/228-9500. Fax 713/223-4528. www.lancaster.com. 93 units. A/C MINIBAR TV TEL. $250–$350 double, $450–$1,000 suite. Children under 18 stay free in parents' room. Weekend rates available, from $130 double. AE, CB, DC, DISC, MC, V. Parking $15.

For those who enjoy the performing arts and nightlife in general, there is no better place to stay in Houston. Within 1 block of the hotel are the symphony, the ballet, the opera, and the Alley Theatre (see chapter 7), and when reserving a room you can have the concierge buy tickets for performances at any of these venues. Also a block away is Bayou Place, where you can catch a movie or a live blues or rock act, and there are many nearby restaurants and nightspots. The hotel occupies a small 12-story building that dates from the 1920s and looks all the smaller for being near the Chase Tower (the tallest skyscraper west of the Mississippi). Rooms are smaller than their counterparts at other downtown hotels but better furnished, reflecting the character of the hotel. Each room includes a queen or king-size bed, easy chair, small writing table, fax machine, VCR, and CD stereo system. Bathrooms are ample and have lots of counter space and bathrobes. Service at the hotel is excellent and includes lots of personal touches such as fresh-cut flowers in the rooms and full ice buckets in the evenings.

Dining/Diversions: The **Bistro Lancaster** is a good choice for dinner and/or drinks before or after the theater. Consequently, it gets a well-dressed crowd.

Amenities: 24-hour room service, 24-hour concierge, fitness room, newspaper, laundry/valet.

EXPENSIVE

Hyatt Regency Houston. 1200 Louisiana St., Houston, TX 77002. ☎ **800/233-1234** or 713/654-1234. Fax 713/658-8606. www.hyatt.com. 963 units. A/C MINIBAR TV TEL. $189–$250 double, $350–$650 suite. Children under 18 stay free in parents' room. Special seasonal, package, and weekend rates available. AE, CB, DC, DISC, JCB, MC, V. Valet parking $18; self-parking $10.

A classic Hyatt hotel with an open, towering atrium lobby accented with glass elevators and ivy draping from the walls, this hotel has remained popular and busy while several other downtown hotels have closed. From its 30 floors, you can see much of the boldest portion of Houston's skyline. The rooms with the best views are along the north side; a still better view can be had from a table in Spindletop, the hotel's spectacular revolving restaurant. The Hyatt is connected to the tunnel system and is in close proximity to most of the major downtown office buildings and city hall. Rooms are not as big as in the Four Seasons but are comfortably furnished, and they offer many amenities, including a writing table with a fax machine. Bathrooms are attractive and well lit.

Dining/Diversions: Three restaurants, lobby bar, and sports bar.

Amenities: Outdoor pool on sixth-floor terrace, fully equipped gym, complimentary shuttle service to downtown destinations and the Galleria, 24-hour room service.

INEXPENSIVE

Days Inn Downtown/Medical Center Area. 4640 South Main St., Houston, TX 77002. ☎ **800/799-9964** or 713/523-3777. Fax 713/523-7501. www.daysinn.com 170 units. A/C TV TEL. $59 double. AE, DC, DISC, MC, V. Free secured parking. The hotel is located where Tex. 59 crosses South Main. If you're on the freeway coming from the north, take the Fannin exit; if coming from the south, take the turnoff (left) for downtown, exit Richmond Ave., then turn right, and then right again on Main.

The best features of this hotel are its proximity to downtown and its price. In fact, this is the cheapest place to stay near downtown. Years ago it was a 280-room Holiday Inn that closed down when this part of Main Street started to decay. Reopened a couple of years ago, the owners have refurbished and made operational 170 of the rooms with plans to open 30 more sometime soon. The common rooms tend toward ugliness, but the large guest rooms are simply and attractively furnished and comfortable. They all have split bathrooms with plenty of counter space. The hotel has a large outdoor pool that is open in the summer, but, at present, there is no restaurant. Though the area around the hotel is seedy, it is not dangerous; a couple of coffee shops and fast-food restaurants are within a block or two. There is a complimentary shuttle to the Medical Center that leaves on demand from 6:30am to 10pm.

2 East End/Near Hobby Airport

MODERATE

Drury Inn & Suites Houston Hobby. 7902 Mosely Rd., Houston, TX 77061. ☎ **800/DRURYINN** or ☎ and fax 713/941-4300. www.drury-inn.com. 134 units. A/C TV TEL. $85 double. Rates include continental breakfast. AE, DC, DISC, MC, V. Free parking. From downtown take I-45 south (Gulf Frwy.), Exit 36 (Airport Blvd.), and turn right on Mosely Rd. If you pass it, make a right on Airport Blvd. and right again onto Mosely.

This hotel is virtually identical (except in price) to the Drury Inn & Suites Near the Galleria, reviewed below in the Uptown section. It's worth your while to check prices here because they are often discounted.

Hilton University of Houston. 4800 Calhoun Rd., Houston, TX 77004. ☎ **800/HOTELUH** or 713/741-2447. Fax 713/743-2472. www.hilton.com. 86 units. A/C TV TEL. $120 double. Children stay free in parents' room. AE, DC, DISC, MC, V. Parking $3.25. To get here from downtown, take I-45 south (Gulf Fwy. toward Galveston), and exit on Calhoun; from Calhoun take right onto University Center Dr. The hotel will be on your left.

This is unlike any other Hilton Hotel in that it is part of the Conrad Hilton College of Hotel and Restaurant Management and is staffed not only by professional full-timers, but also by students performing their lab work. It deserves consideration because of its rates, which often drop significantly when there are no academic conferences or parents' weekends; its location on the University of Houston campus between downtown and the attractions in Houston's southeast side; and its service, which is often excellent. Rooms throughout the hotel's eight floors are large L-shaped layouts, with modern furnishings that include a sleeper sofa with coffee table. Bathrooms are large and have lots of counter space. Extras include data ports and the daily weekday paper. **Eric's,** the hotel's restaurant, is far better than most hotel restaurants and offers a menu with a Latin flair. There is also a large health club with pool next to the hotel that guests can use for free.

INEXPENSIVE

Red Carpet Inn Hobby Regency Motor Lodge. 6161 Gulf Freeway, Houston, TX 77023. ☎ **800/928-2871** or 713/928-2871. Fax. 713/928-3050. 150 units. A/C TV TEL. $37–$43.50 double. Weekly rates available. AE, MC, V. Free off-street parking. Take the Wayside exit (41-B) off the Gulf Freeway.

Nice and cheap and with its own peculiar character, this hotel offers the most lodging for the buck of any place on this side of town. The rooms are medium-sized with 1970s-style cheap furniture, but they're clean and comfortable and come with cable TV. A large outdoor pool is open in season. The real character of the place comes from the **Fajita Haven Restaurant** and the **Pu San Lounge.** The former is a sterling example of a roadside Tex-Mex joint with all the requisite dishes; the latter is the archetypal Houston neighborhood blue-collar bar with red carpet that smells slightly of stale beer. The bar has a friendly staff, a pool table, dartboards, and a TV always tuned to sports.

3 South Main

EXPENSIVE

Hilton Houston Plaza. 6833 Travis St., Houston, TX 77030. ☎ **800/HILTONS** or 713/313-4000. Fax 713/313-4660. www.houstonplaza.hilton.com. 181 units. A/C MINIBAR TV TEL. $145 double, $165 suite. Weekend rates available. AE, DC, DISC, MC, V. Valet parking $14; self-parking $8.

In terms of amenities, service, and location, this is the best of the hotels around the Medical Center. Consequently, it enjoys a high occupancy rate, especially with people attending medical conferences. As the occupancy rate increases, so do the prices (well above those quoted here). Try to book early and, if you have any flexibility, get rates for different dates. Making matters worse for travelers on a budget is the small number of standard rooms, only 40 out of 181.

The hotel's facilities—a lovely ninth-floor pool and sunning terrace, a large state-of-the-art gym with saunas and whirlpools, and a well-equipped business center—set this hotel apart from neighboring hotels. The large rooms are comfortable and well furnished, and include extras such as a minifridge and wet bar. The building is 19 stories tall, with views toward either the Medical Center or Rice University; it's a toss-up as to which is prettier. The hotel's location on the rim of the Medical Center is actually an advantage over its principal Medical Center rivals (a Marriott and a Crowne Plaza) because it makes getting to and from the hotel much easier, avoiding the Medical Center traffic congestion and the tight parking garages.

Dining/Diversions: One restaurant serving international food and a small lobby bar.

Amenities: Complimentary shuttle service to the nearby museums and shopping areas and any location within the Medical Center, 24-hour room service, a large, outdoor, heated pool open most of the year with a large sunning deck, well-equipped gym with locker rooms and separate saunas and whirlpools, a business center with computers.

✪ **Park Plaza Warwick.** 5701 South Main St., Houston, TX 77005. ☎ **800/822-PARK** or 713/526-1991. Fax 713/526-0359. 308 units. A/C TV TEL. $159–$199 double, $189–$450 suite. Extra person $10. Children under 12 stay free in parents' room. AE, CB, DC, DISC, ER, JCB, MC, V. Valet parking $15; self-parking $8.

At one time, the Warwick was *the* luxury hotel in Houston. Over the years, it has lost its premier ranking but not its charm or its enviable location on the most attractive part of South Main Street in the middle of the Museum District and near the Montrose Area. Rooms throughout its 12 stories have lots of windows and offer good views in any direction. Some come with one or two double beds, others with a king bed, and still others with two queen beds. Most of the rooms are large; all come furnished in period-style, predominantly French pieces. The bathrooms are medium-sized and come with ample counter space.

Dining/Diversions: Two restaurants, the **Hunt Room** (formal) and the **Terrace Café** (informal), offer international cuisine. The Terrace Café doubles as a lobby bar and offers a charming view of the art museum's garden across Main Street from the hotel.

Amenities: An enticing terrace pool bordered by palm trees, exercise room and saunas, reservations at Tour 18 Golf Course or the nearby Hermann Park Golf Course, concierge, 24-hour in-room dining, complimentary weekday newspaper, laundry/dry cleaning.

MODERATE

Holiday Inn Hotel and Suites Houston Medical Center. 6800 Main St., Houston, TX 77035. ☎ **800/HOLIDAY** or 713/528-7744. Fax 713/528-6983. www.holiday-inn.com. 285 units. A/C TV TEL. $120–$150 double, $150–$175 suite. Medical rates for hospital outpatients available. AE, CB, DC, DISC, EC, ER, JCB, MC, V. Free parking.

This hotel can be a bargain. Spot checks on prices turned up a number of instances when standard rates were floating well below the published rack rates. The hotel has an excellent location across from the Medical Center, at the intersection with Holcombe Boulevard. Rooms are comfortable but furnished with little effort to hide their hotel-like character. All include a worktable, modem hook-up, and an in-room safe. Some suites have full kitchens. What's not to like is the shortage of staff at the front desk and in guest services that makes getting attended to an exercise in patience.

The hotel has a restaurant that will work for breakfast if you're not in a hurry, a lobby bar, a guest lounge, a pool, and a small fitness room. Services on the premises include a hair salon, travel services, free Internet access, a free shuttle to Medical Center locations, museums, and shopping in the Village or the Galleria.

La Quinta Inn Astrodome. 9911 Buffalo Speedway (at Loop 610), Houston, TX 77054. ☎ **800/531-5900** or 713/668-8082. Fax 713/668-0821. www.laquinta.com. 115 units. A/C MINIBAR TV TEL. $80 double. Rates include continental breakfast. Children under 18 stay free in parents' room. AE, CB, DC, DISC, MC, V. Free parking.

This two-story motel is just down the road from AstroWorld and WaterWorld. The rooms include extras like free local calls and 25-inch TVs that are larger than what you usually find in hotels in this price range. You also get well-lit, spacious bathrooms. The furniture and decoration are the result of a recent renovation that succeeded in making the rooms comfortable and attractive, albeit unmistakably motel-like. More important is the fact that they shield out the noise from the freeway. There is a medium-size outdoor pool on the grounds, but no restaurant.

Patrician Bed & Breakfast Inn. 1200 Southmore Blvd., Houston, TX 77004. ☎ 800/553-5797 or 713/523-1114. Fax 713/523-0790. www.texasbnb. com. 4 units. A/C TV TEL. $95–$115 double, $130 suite. Rates include full breakfast. AE, DC, DISC, MC, V. Free parking. Located on the corner of Southmore and

San Jacinto not far from Tex. 59. San Jacinto is a one-way street heading north that runs parallel to Main St. 2 blocks to the east.

This is a smart choice for those who want a location near the Museum District that's also not far from downtown. Lovely wood floors, lots of area rugs, a few period pieces, old-fashioned wallpaper—you'll definitely get the B&B experience, but not in its most gussied-up aspect. Patricia Thomas, the owner, gives equal emphasis to comfort and convenience. All rooms come with queen-size beds, cable TV and terry cloth robes. The two large doubles are quite spacious with ample bathrooms that sport claw-foot tubs with shower fixtures; the one on the first floor also offers a large desk, which makes it attractive to the business traveler. With its proximity to downtown and convenient parking, this B&B gets a number of businesspeople on the weekdays.

INEXPENSIVE

Astrodome Medical Center Hotel. 9000 South Main, Houston, TX 77025. ☎ and fax **713/666-4151.** 93 units. A/C TV TEL. $55 double. Rates include continental breakfast. AE, MC, V. Free off-street parking.

This is a simple hotel with two stories of rooms lining a large parking lot. The quietest rooms are the ones at the back of the property; the front ones can be noisy. The rooms have simple painted-wood furniture and two full-size beds; most come with a small fridge and a microwave, which makes them a value for people wanting save money on dining. Bathrooms are clean but a little small. There's a complimentary shuttle to the major hospitals in the Medical Center that leaves every hour. There is talk of a name change for the hotel, so look for the address rather than the name.

✪ **Grant Palm Court Inn.** 8200 South Main (just south of intersection with Kirby), Houston, TX 77025. ☎ **800/255-8904** or 713/668-8000. Fax 713/668-7777. 64 units. A/C TV TEL. $39–$46 double. Rates include continental breakfast. AE, MC, V. Free off-street parking with spaces for larger vehicles.

This is the best lodgings bargain in Houston: attractive, immaculate rooms on well-kept grounds at astonishingly low rates. The higher rate is for rooms with two full-size beds that can accommodate up to four people at no extra charge. All rooms are quiet and are comparable to rooms costing twice as much at many other hotels. The rooms occupy a couple of two-story buildings separated by lovely grounds that hold a pool, a Jacuzzi, and a wading pool. There is also a laundry room, but no restaurant. The front desk leases VCRs and can lend guests irons and ironing boards. The hotel is close to both the Medical Center and the Astrodome/AstroWorld complex. As with all hotels in this part of Houston, you must reserve well in advance for February, when the rodeo comes to town.

4 Montrose

VERY EXPENSIVE

✪ **La Colombe d'Or.** 3410 Montrose Blvd., Houston, TX 77006. ☎ **713/ 524-7999.** Fax 713/524-8923. www.lacolombedor.com. 6 units. A/C TV TEL. $195–$275 suite, $575 penthouse. AE, DC, DISC, MC, V. Free valet parking. Located 3 blocks south of Westheimer Rd. at the corner of Harold St.

If you enjoy the smallness of scale of a B&B and the fact that the rooms don't look like typical hotel rooms, but you want more space, more service, and more privacy, this is the hotel for you. The five suites are extremely large, with hardwood floors, area rugs, antiques, king-size beds, and large bathrooms with marble tile. Some suites come with separate dining rooms, and the in-room dining is one of the things this hotel is known for. The original mansion that the hotel occupies was built in the 1920s for oilman Walter Fondren. The interior has some beautiful architectural features, and its location puts you close to the museums, the restaurants, and the downtown area.

Dining/Diversions: The hotel restaurant offers a choice of four different dining rooms, serves French cuisine, and is praised by local dining critics. Coat and tie are required for men. The bar makes for a cozy, softly lit setting for a drink, or you can have drinks served in your room.

Amenities: Hair dryers, irons and ironing boards are available for the asking. In-room dining is available until 10pm on weekdays, 11pm on weekends.

MODERATE

Allen Park Inn. 2121 Allen Pkwy., Houston, TX 77019. ☎ **800/231-6310** or 713/521-9321. Fax 713/521-9321. www.allenparkinn.com. 242 units. A/C TV TEL. $108–$118 double, $135–$250 suite. Extra person $10. Children under 10 stay free in parents' room. AE, CB, DC, DISC, MC, V. Free outdoor parking. Located 1 block east of the intersection of Montrose Blvd. and Allen Pkwy.

This is a quirky place that's not easy to categorize: It's part hotel, part motel, and has unexpected offerings such as an in-house barber shop, a very large and beautifully tended lawn with beds of flowers and rose bushes, and a restaurant that time forgot. The location, fronting Buffalo Bayou in plain sight of downtown, makes Allen Park Inn perfect for anyone wanting to be centrally located, especially those who like to run or walk and will enjoy the trails that line both sides of the bayou. Most of the rooms are grouped motel-style in long, two-story buildings. The décor is something of a 1970s throwback and the rooms could use a little more light, but they are quiet, comfortable, and include amenities such as a small writing table. On one side of the property is a newer three-story building that holds better-lit rooms, but I prefer the look of the original ones. The hotel offers two restaurants and a bar, a poolside bar, a large pool in the midst of the lush grounds, room service until 2am, and laundry.

Lovett Inn. 501 Lovett Blvd., Houston, TX 77006. ☎ **800/779-5224** or 713/ 522-5224. Fax 713/528-6708. www.lovettinn.com. 12 units, 8 with private bathroom. A/C TV TEL. $75–$85 double with shared bathroom; $115–$150 double with private bathroom. Rates include continental breakfast. AE, DISC, MC, V. Off-street parking for 6 cars. From the corner of Westheimer and Montrose, head east (toward town) on Westeimer 4 blocks to Taft and turn right; Lovett will be the first street. Turn right again, and the Inn is in the middle of the block on the south side.

One block off Westheimer and 3 blocks from Montrose Boulevard, the Inn offers plenty of quiet, without being far from the busy restaurant and club district of the Montrose Area. The house dates from the early 1900s and was built by one of Houston's mayors. Rooms in the main house are spacious and well furnished with period furniture, wood floors, area rugs, and none of the cutesiness that so many B&Bs feel obliged to deliver. Larger and more modern rooms are in buildings in back of the main house; they have separate entrances that offer greater privacy and additional amenities such as a refrigerator, microwave, wet bar, and whirlpool tubs. A swimming pool, patio, library, and dining room are also available to guests.

5 Kirby District

EXPENSIVE

Renaissance Houston Hotel. 6 Greenway Plaza East, Houston, TX 77046. ☎ **800/HOTELS-1** or 713/629-1200. www.renaissancehotels.com. 388 units. A/C TV TEL. $189–$199 double, $350–$1,200 suite. Weekend rates available. Children under 18 stay free in parents' room. AE, CB, DC, DISC, JCB, MC, V. Valet parking $14; self-parking $8.

The only hotel in the Greenway Plaza (though there are a few nearby), this 20-story hotel enjoys access to Greenway's office buildings through its concourse level of shops, a food court, post office, Fed Ex office, and a movie theater. It is also connected to the Houston City Club by another walkway, and hotel guests can enjoy the use of its facilities including indoor tennis courts, racquetball, and jogging track. Also next door is the Compaq Center, Houston's sports arena for basketball and hockey. The hotel's location off the Southwest Freeway means quick access to either downtown or Uptown.

Rooms on the concierge floors offer extra services like complimentary continental breakfast and evening cocktails. All standard rooms are spacious and decorated in an eclectic style, which makes them a bit more interesting than your standard humdrum hotel room. Rooms come with a king or queen-size bed or two queen-size beds, an easy chair and ottoman, a writing table, and attractive bathrooms.

Dining/Diversions: One full-service restaurant, a sports bar for sandwiches and drinks, and a relaxing lobby bar.

Amenities: Outdoor pool and Jacuzzi, well-equipped exercise room with locker rooms and sauna, business center, complimentary newspaper, complimentary shuttle for trips within 3-mile radius, 24-hour room service, laundry.

MODERATE

Doubletree Club Houston Near Greenway Plaza. 2828 Southwest Freeway, Houston, TX 77098. ☎ **800/222-8733** or 713/942-2111. Fax 713/942-9934. www.doubletreehotels.com. 216 units. A/C TV TEL. $129 double. AE, CB, DC, DISC, MC, V. Free parking.

This is a businessperson's hotel that's comfortable and well situated. It has easy access to the freeway, which leads either downtown or toward the Galleria, both just a few minutes away. Spot checks showed substantially discounted rates, so it's worth a call. Rooms are spacious; some have sofa sleepers. Furnishings are modern and functional without looking cheap. There's plenty of light and a good-size writing table, two phones with data ports, free local calls, and medium-size bathrooms. The hotel has a ground-floor pool and fitness room, as well as an **Au Bon Pain** cafe.

6   Uptown (Galleria/Post Oak)

VERY EXPENSIVE

Doubletree Guest Suites. 5353 Westheimer Rd., Houston, TX 77056. ☎ **800/ 222-TREE** or 713/961-9000. Fax 713/877-8835. www.doubletreehotels.com. 335 suites. A/C MINIBAR TV TEL. $200 1-bedroom suite; $299 2-bedroom suite. AE, CB, DC, DISC, MC, V. Valet parking $15; self-parking $8.

This 26-story hotel, 1 block west of the Galleria shopping complex, offers large, plainly furnished suites, each with a fully equipped kitchen (with microwave and dishwasher) and a dining area for four people. The hotel is well priced, gets a lot of repeat business, and is a favorite for extended stays. The sitting room includes a sofa or two and armchairs, and a large TV. The bedroom includes two full-size beds, a writing table with phone and data port, and a medium-size TV. Bathrooms are large with plenty of counter space. The service here is quite good.

Dining/Diversions: A bar and grill that specializes in American food.

Amenities: Outdoor pool and hot tub, small fitness room with weight machine and several aerobic machines, laundry room, convenience store, 24-hour room service (limited menu after 11pm), concierge, business services, laundry/dry cleaning service, free shuttle transportation within 3-mile radius, free weekday paper, free coffee and tea in each suite.

JW Marriott Hotel by the Galleria. 5150 Westheimer Rd., Houston, TX 77056. ☎ **713/961-1500.** Fax 713/599-2102. www.marriotthotels.com. 514 units. A/C MINIBAR TV TEL. $249 double. AE, CB, DC, DISC, JCB, MC, V. Valet parking $18; self-parking $9 in garage, free in open lot.

On Westheimer facing the Galleria, this luxury high-rise hotel offers lots of amenities and central location. Rooms are smaller than at the Westin hotels but are packed with features, and the Marriott has more recreation and leisure facilities. Rooms come with a writing table, two phone lines, three phones, high-speed Internet connections, medium-size TV, and a smaller TV in the dressing area. Bathrooms are well lit and come with make-up mirrors and terry cloth robes. The décor is nothing spectacular, but at least it isn't ugly. Avoid reserving a room on the fifth floor, where the health club is located.

Dining/Diversions: A large restaurant specializing in Southwestern cooking but also serving traditional American dishes. Attractive lobby bar.

Amenities: A full-service health club offering a very large gym loaded with state-of-the-art equipment, locker rooms and showers, unisex sauna and steam rooms, small indoor/ outdoor pool, Jacuzzi, large sunning deck, racquetball and basketball courts, massage service. There's also a full-service business center and a hair salon. Services include concierge, same-day laundry, free morning coffee in lobby, room service until midnight offering, among other things, Pizza Hut pizzas.

✪ **Omni Houston Hotel.** 4 Riverway, Houston, TX 77056. ☎ **800/ THE-OMNI** or 713/871-8181. Fax 713/871-8116. 373 units. A/C MINIBAR TV TEL. $229–$350 double, $259–$809 suite. Children under 18 stay free in parents' room. AE, CB, DC, DISC, JCB, MC, V. Valet parking $15; outdoor self-parking free.

This hotel is an island of tranquility in Uptown's sea of commotion. Flanking it on one side is a broad expanse of lawn with a decorative pool fed by cascading water and adorned with a small troop of black swans; on the other side is the heavily wooded Memorial Park. You'd think that you're miles from the busy Uptown malls, but you're not. In contrast to the modern exterior of this 11-story building—angular lines, bold colors, stark surfaces—the guest rooms are pictures of traditionalism, with 18th-century–style furniture, damask and brocade upholstery, wallpaper, and bedspreads with flounces in neoclassical patterns. The rooms are large and come with a view of either Memorial Park with downtown in the background or of the pools, the lawn, and the black swans. Each room includes a CD player, two phones with data port, and writing table. The large bathrooms come with make-up mirrors, good counter space, and bathrobes.

Dining/Diversions: La Reserve (for which you should make la reservation) is a formal restaurant open for dinner and serving continental food. **Café on the Green** is a casual restaurant serving breakfast, lunch, and dinner. There is a lobby bar that is quiet and comfortable, and a basement pub with a DJ and dance floor.

Amenities: Two large pools with underwater music (one is heated) and poolside food service during the season, four tennis courts, fitness room with hot tub, locker rooms with

🏨 Family-Friendly Hotels

Omni Houston Hotel *(see p. 50)*   With its Omni Kids Club, this hotel makes a special effort to keep smaller children amused. Kids receive a packet of goodies at check in, and parents can even request a small, pretend suitcase that holds more games and such. As part of the program, the concierge can organize activities and trips for children to places such as the zoo.

Grant Palm Court Inn *(see p. 45)*   This little economy motel allows children to stay at no extra cost and has a wading pool and small playscape area. It's also situated close to AstroWorld and WaterWorld, of interest to older kids.

separate saunas, business center, complimentary newspaper, full-service spa, Omni Kids Club, 24-hour room service and concierge, laundry/valet.

Sheraton Suites Houston near the Galleria. 2400 West Loop South, Houston, TX 77027. ☎ **888/321-4733** or 713/586-2444. Fax 713/586-2445. www.sheraton.com/suiteshouston. 286 suites. A/C MINIBAR TV TEL. $229 suite. AE, CB, DC, DISC, EC, JCB, MC, V. Valet parking $15; self-parking $10.

The rooms at this all-suite hotel are attractive and show more character than most hotel rooms. The headboards and accents are postmodern, and the granite countertops are snazzy. These suites are not as big as the suites at the Doubletree Guest Suites, but they are in many ways more comfortable and more attractive. The pillow-top beds come in two full-size or one king. An easy-to-use retractable door makes the living room and bedroom usable as one large space or as two separate rooms with the ample bathroom accessible from either. Amenities include two phone lines, high-speed Internet connection, and wet bar. The best rooms face westward, away from Loop 610. There are 18 "smart suites" that include more business features, such as a fax machine, and luxuries, such as bathrobes. The service here is attentive and personal. One caveat: If you like to read in bed, this hotel is not for you; the bedside lights are much too dim.

Dining/Diversions: One restaurant serves dishes from a simple, well-conceived menu featuring grilled specialties, and there's a quiet, relaxing bar.

Amenities: Small outdoor pool, small Jacuzzi, fitness room equipped with more aerobic equipment than weight machines. Services include in-room dining from 6pm to midnight, and concierge.

⭘ **Westin Galleria and Westin Oaks.** 5060 W. Alabama and 5011 Westeimer Rd., Houston, TX 77056. ☎ **800/WESTIN-1** or 713/960-8100. Fax 713/960-6553 (Westin Galleria) or 713/960-6554 (Westin Oaks). www.westin.com. 893 units. A/C MINIBAR TV TEL. $215–$225 double, $425 suite. AE, CB, DC, DISC, EC, JCB, MC, V. Valet parking $19; self-parking free.

These two hotels, and only these two, are part and parcel of the Galleria complex. You can walk straight from the hotel lobby into the mall without ever leaving the great indoors. Either of these should be the first choice for dedicated shoppers, and a good choice for anyone wishing to be in the Uptown area. Similar in size, name, and appearance, they are often confused. The Westin Oaks towers 20 stories above the northeast side of the mall, is closest to the freeway (Loop 610), and faces Westheimer Road from across the mall's broad parking lot. It is a family hotel and has no alcoholic beverages in the minibars. The rooms have been redecorated and cost $10 more per night than at the Westin Galleria. Only a few floors taller, the Westin Galleria is on the southwest side of the Galleria, and is connected to the mall's first addition (Galleria II). It is more of a hotel for business travelers, offering a business center and more formal dining than the Westin Oaks.

Other than these differences, staying in one is much like staying in the other. The rooms in both hotels are large, with similar features except that the Oaks has newer furniture. Two features of these hotels bear special mention: One is their highly touted beds (they come with their own trademark name), which, all hype aside, are very comfortable; the other feature is the balconies, a luxury that is becoming more and more scarce in high-rise hotels. There is nothing fancy about these balconies, and every room has one, but they add greatly to the enjoyment of staying here. From them you can watch all the hustle and bustle below while in complete serenity, and you can take in the impressive views of the modern skyline that surrounds the Galleria. At the Westin Oaks, you must ask for a room facing north, but at the Westin Galleria get one facing south. Hotel staff is very attentive. One detail somewhat at odds with a hotel of this category is that the hallways are a bit shabby.

Dining/Diversions: Formal restaurant serving Italian food with an American flair and a comfortable, quiet bar (Westin Galleria); informal restaurant serving comfort food, and a sports bar (Westin Oaks).

Amenities: Concierge, business center (Westin Galleria only), 24-hour room service, heated outdoor swimming pools, tennis courts, access to health club.

MODERATE

Drury Inn & Suites Near the Galleria. Post Oak Park at West Loop South, Houston, TX 77027. ☎ **800/DRURY-INN** or ☎ and fax 713/963-0700. www.drury-inn.com. 126 units. A/C TV TEL. $102 double. Rates include continental breakfast. AE, DC, DISC, MC, V. Free parking. Pets accepted with $25 deposit.

If you cross to the other side of Loop 610, room prices fall considerably even though the hotels are only a couple of blocks farther from the Galleria. One of the best lodging values in this area is this Drury Inn. Rooms are medium-size and comfortable, with extra-long double beds, perfect for tall folk. Instead of the usual easy chair and ottoman, there is a recliner; the TV is larger than normal and receives the usual cable channels. While the bathroom is of okay size, it offers limited counter space. The hotel doesn't have a restaurant, but it offers free evening cocktails from Monday through Thursday. On the premises there is a small indoor/outdoor pool, a Jacuzzi, a fitness room, and a laundry room. Hotel guests also have the use of a nearby health club.

La Quinta Inn & Suites Galleria. 1625 West Loop South (Galleria area at San Felipe), Houston, TX 77027. ☎ **800/687-6667** or 713/355-3440. Fax 713/355-2990. www.laquinta.com. 173 units. A/C TV TEL. $112–$122 double, $147 suite. Children under 18 stay free in parents' room. Rates include complimentary breakfast. AE, DC, DISC, MC, V. Free parking.

You can tell at first glance that this immaculately clean inn, constructed in 1998, is a new breed of La Quinta, with a gurgling fountain in the lobby, a fitness room, and a fairly large outdoor heated pool with separate hot tub. There's also a laundry room and same-day dry cleaning service. Close proximity to the shopping along Post Oak and in the Galleria seals the deal. Standard rooms come with two double beds; the "King Plus" room comes with king-size bed and a recliner. There is something unmistakably motel-like about the furnishings and some rooms smell of cleaning solution.

7 The Heights

MODERATE

Sara's Bed and Breakfast Inn. 941 Heights Blvd., Houston, TX 77008. ☎ **800/593-1130** or 713/868-1130. Fax 713/868-3284. www.saras.com. 13 units (11 with private bathroom). A/C TV TEL. $70–$125 double, $105–$150 suite. AE, CB, DC, DISC, JCB, MC, V. Twelve free off-road parking spots. No children under age 12. The house is between 9th and 10th sts. on Heights Blvd. From I-10 take the Heights Blvd. exit and turn north. From the Montrose area, take Waugh, which becomes Heights after going under I-10.

For the traditional B&B experience—period décor, themed rooms, beautifully furnished common rooms—this is the place to stay. Sara's occupies a large Texas Victorian house in the Heights. It is immaculately kept and brightly decorated. Most rooms come with a queen or a king bed; some come with a full or a king and a full. Several of the rooms are inspired by other cities of Texas, including Fort Worth, San Antonio, Galveston. The hosts serve a full breakfast, and a stay here is delightful.

8 Near Bush Intercontinental Airport

EXPENSIVE

Houston Airport Marriott. 18700 JFK Blvd., Houston, TX 77032. ☎ **800/228-2290** or 281/443-2310. Fax 281/443-5294. www.marriott.com. 566 units. A/C TV TEL. $195 double. AE, CB, DC, DISC, ER, JCB, MC, V. Free self-parking.

Don't let the address fool you—this hotel is not on "Hotel Row." It's located smack dab in the middle of the airport itself between terminals B and C, and it's on the airport tram line, which means no messing with taxis, shuttle buses, or rental cars. With this enviable location, the hotel gets a lot of business conferences. The revolving rooftop restaurant adds to the hotel's popularity—you'll see planes landing and taking off with a view that is pretty much the same as that of the airport's control tower. Guest rooms at the hotel are large and attractively furnished. The bathrooms are not particularly big, but the beds are comfortable, and everything else about the room is great.

Dining/Diversions: The revolving rooftop restaurant is a lovely place for dinner, served from 5:30 to 10pm (and lunch is served for conference attendees). There's an American grill open for breakfast, lunch, and dinner as well as a rooftop bar.

Amenities: Outdoor swimming pool open year-round; outdoor, sheltered Jacuzzi; large gym with lots of equipment for aerobic workouts; room service until midnight, including Pizza Hut pizzas; free transportation to airport via underground tram.

MODERATE

Wingate Inn. 15615 JFK Blvd., Houston, TX 77032. ☎ **800/228-1000** or 281/987-8777. Fax 281/987-9317. www.wingateinns.com. 101 units. A/C TV TEL. $89 double; weekend rates $59 double. Rates include continental breakfast. Children under 18 stay free in parents' room. AE, CB, DC, DISC, MC, V. Free parking. From the airport, follow signs pointing to Beltway 8 and I-45; they will guide you onto JFK Blvd. From the city, take either I-45 or Tex. 59 (the Eastex freeway) to Beltway 8; from there follow signs to the airport.

As far as airport hotels go, this one has the most extras for the buck. Rooms are large, comfortable, and well equipped, including T1 Internet connections, two phone lines (including a cordless phone) with free local calls, large writing table, minifridge, microwave, and in-room safe. Services include free airport shuttle and continental breakfast (even though there's no restaurant). There's a 24-hour business center, a small outdoor pool, a small but up-to-date fitness room, and an indoor Jacuzzi.

5

Dining

*T*he Houston restaurant scene, like the city itself, is cosmopolitan. The primary influences come from Louisiana, Mexico, and Southeast Asia, but you can find restaurants serving just about any cuisine you can think of. There are several that serve continental cuisine, including Tony's, an institution among Houston's wealthy and perhaps known more for the people who go there than for the food served. What constitutes Houston's native cooking is well represented by barbecue, soul food, Tex-Mex joints, and steak houses.

1 Downtown/Midtown

VERY EXPENSIVE

✪ **Brennan's.** 3300 Smith (corner with Stuart). ☎ **713/522-9711.** Reservations recommended. Main courses $27–$32. AE, DC, DISC, MC, V. Mon–Fri 11:30am–2pm, 5:45–10pm; Sat 11am–2pm, 5:45–10pm; Sun 10am–2pm, 5:45–10pm. After Smith St. crosses Elgin/Westheimer, look for the restaurant on your right. Be careful not to pass it or you will get fed onto the Southwest Freeway and won't be able to exit until Shepherd St. SOUTHERN/CREOLE.

Fine dining a la New Orleans: Brennan's opened in 1967 as a sister restaurant to the famous New Orleans original, and it's a perennial favorite on most local "Top Restaurant" lists. The various dining rooms are strikingly elegant (I don't think you'll find a lovelier table in all of Houston), the service is superb, and the menu will be new territory to all but those coming from Louisiana. The selection of dishes varies daily but usually has a few classic Creole specialties such as roux-less seafood gumbo or its well-known turtle soup. Brennan's is also known for is its chef's table, which is located in the restaurant's kitchen. The table must be reserved far in advance and can accommodate between 4 and 10 people at $75 per person. For that price, guests are treated to several of the chef's special creations right as they come off the stove.

EXPENSIVE

Liberty Noodle. 909-E Texas Ave. ☎ **713/222-2695.** Main courses $8–$24; lunch $8–$13. AE, DC, DISC, MC, V. Mon–Fri 11am–2:30pm and 5–10pm (until 11pm Wed–Thurs, midnight Fri); Sat 11am–midnight. PAN-ASIAN.

At night, this is clearly the feeding ground for Houston's young, smart set. The restaurant is located on the ground floor of the old Rice Hotel, now one of the hottest addresses in the city, and many diners show up from the nearby theater district. You can dine outdoors under the old hotel's original cast-iron canopy, or in the slightly cramped dining room, decorated with Asian and modern sparseness. Asian noodle dishes are finding a warm reception by those who want quick food that's not fried or too fatty but still has flavor. The most popular dishes here are the spicy noodles with beef, chicken, or tofu, the spicy coconut soup (delicious), and duck noodles. The restaurant uses mostly rice noodles for its dishes, but, at times, will use Japanese noodles. Vegetarian substitutions can be made for any dish. At lunch, the prices are substantially lower, and the crowd is more of the office worker variety.

MODERATE

Mai's. 3403 Milam. ☎ **713/520-7684.** Reservations recommended on weekends. Main courses $6–$16. AE, DC, DISC, MC, V. Mon–Thurs 10am–3am; Fri–Sat 10am–4am. From downtown take Milam, which parallels Main St. 2 blocks to the west. VIETNAMESE.

Occupying a two-story brick building with green awnings on Milam just south of downtown, Mai's is the last of a half-dozen Vietnamese restaurants you'll pass in the preceding 6 blocks. In several ways it is the best choice, but it should not be thought of as having a lock on good Vietnamese food. I do, however, appreciate its dependability and the long hours it keeps because you never know when you might get a yen for a bowl of Vietnamese noodles (and they're all good). At Mai's, you can not only get noodles (listed as vermicelli or bun), but you can also have *pho,* the national dish, a soup to which you add several vegetables and herbs. Sample the ever-popular spring and summer rolls served with nam pla and/or peanut sauce, and try a chicken stir-fry with chile and lemongrass, or the garlic chicken or charcoal-roasted beef with lemongrass. If you're in Houston for any time at all, try to make it to a Vietnamese restaurant at least once. Houston's Vietnamese population is very large, and it has made an indelible imprint on the city's dining scene.

Central Houston Dining

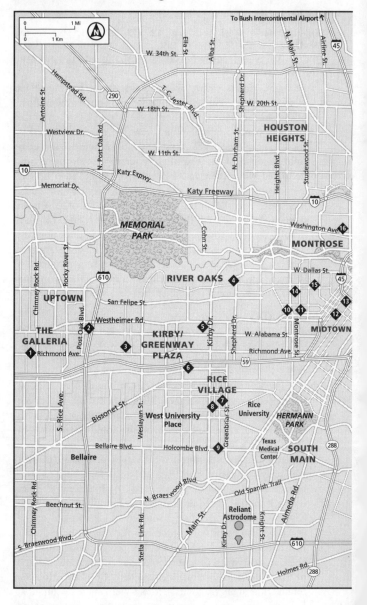

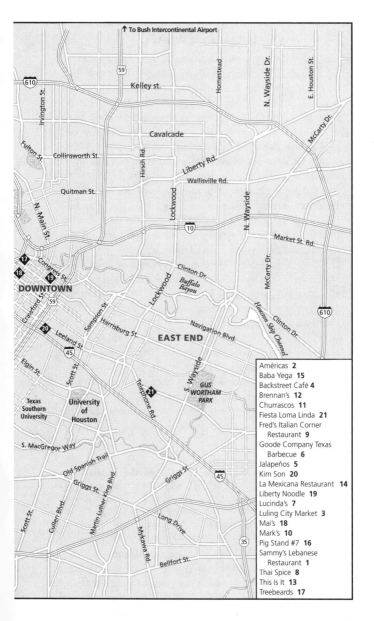

↑ To Bush Intercontinental Airport

610

59

Kelley st.

Irvington St.

Fulton St.

Collinsworth St.

Quitman St.

N. Main St.

Cavalcade

Hirsch Rd.

Liberty Rd.

Wallisville Rd.

Lockwood

Homestead

N. Wayside Dr.

E. Houston St.

McCarty Dr.

N. Wayside

10

Market St. Rd.

McCarty Dr.

610

17

18

Congress St.

Clinton Dr.

19

DOWNTOWN

Crawford St.

59

Lockwood

Buffalo Bayou

Clinton Dr.

Houston Ship Channel

20

Leeland St.

Sampson St.

Harrisburg St.

45

EAST END

Navigation Blvd.

Elgin St.

Scott St.

S. Wayside

Texas Southern University

University of Houston

21

GUS WORTHAM PARK

Telephone Rd.

S. MacGregor Way

Old Spanish Trail

Griggs St.

45

Griggs St.

Scott St.

Cullen Blvd.

Martin Luther King Blvd.

Mykawa Rd.

Long Drive

35

Bellfort St.

Américas **2**
Baba Yega **15**
Backstreet Café **4**
Brennan's **12**
Churrascos **11**
Fiesta Loma Linda **21**
Fred's Italian Corner
   Restaurant **9**
Goode Company Texas
   Barbecue **6**
Jalapeños **5**
Kim Son **20**
La Mexicana Restaurant **14**
Liberty Noodle **19**
Lucinda's **7**
Luling City Market **3**
Mai's **18**
Mark's **10**
Pig Stand #7 **16**
Sammy's Lebanese
   Restaurant **1**
Thai Spice **8**
This Is It **13**
Treebeards **17**

Fast Food a la Houston

We all know that it often becomes necessary to find a meal that can be had quickly, conveniently, and cheaply. You can do this in Houston without having to suffer at the hands of the national fast food chains, where the food tastes pretty much the same whether you're in Houston or Honolulu. Houston has a number of local chains that do a good job of cooking up fast food with character and local flavor. Here are a few to consider:

James Coney Island Hot Dogs started up in Houston in the 1930s at its present downtown location. It's famous for its bowls of dark, rich, meaty chili and its original chilidogs. (Most Houstonians consider hot dogs without chili as either unful-filled potential or foreign novelty.) You can order the chili with or without beans or as a chili pie. For hot dogs, I recommend the original Coney or the Texas Chilidog without cheese. There are 22 locations around Houston, including downtown (815 Dallas St.), in the Kirby District (3607 Shepherd at the corner of Richmond), around the Galleria area (5745 Westheimer), and out along the Gulf Freeway (6955 Gulf Fwy. and 10600 Gulf Fwy.).

In 1962 the Antone family, originally from Lebanon, opened an exotic import grocery store on Taft Street near Allen Parkway called **Antone's.** There they introduced Houston to their now famous Po'boy (sub) sandwiches, which caught on in a big way. For lunch, you can't go wrong with one of these, which come already prepared. Get the original Green Label or

INEXPENSIVE

Pig Stand #7. 2412 Washington Ave. ☎ **713/864-4041.** Reservations not accepted. Main courses $5–$10. AE, DISC, MC, V. Mon–Thurs 6am–7:30pm; Fri–Sat 6am–10pm; Sun 7am–8pm. From downtown, take Congress or Franklin west until they feed onto Washington; look for the restaurant on the right a couple of minutes down the road. From the Montrose Area take Montrose Blvd. north over the bayou and turn right on Washington. TEXAN/AMERICAN.

What indeed can be said of a place that defines itself as the "Home of the Pig Sandwich"? A place where totemic pig art in all its many genres (more than you can imagine) festoons the joint from floor to ceiling? And then consider that the entire collection of "pigaphenalia" was acquired over the years the super Red Label, both of which are a combination of ham, salami, cheese, pickles, and special chow-chow on fresh baked bread. Antone's locations include 807 Taft (close to downtown), 2424 Dunstan (in the Village), 8110 Kirby (across from the Astrodome complex), 1440 S. Voss (at San Felipe, about a mile out from the Galleria), and 3823 Bellaire (at Stella Link, west of the Medical Center).

Beck's Prime is a local chain of upscale burger joints that is known for excellent big juicy burgers and great shakes. Locations include 2902 Kirby Dr. (at Westheimer), inside the Galleria, and at 910 Travis (in the downtown tunnel system below Bank One Center).

Café Express operates under the guiding principle that fast food can be nutritious, fresh, and cooked with at least some artistry. The owner of the chain is the chef at Café Annie's, a very expensive and popular restaurant in the Uptown area that is often at the top of the list of Houston's fine dining spots. Specialties at Café Express include a variety of salads, lively pasta dishes, juicy roast chicken, and a large bar of condiments that includes olives, olive oil, peppers, mustards, and vinegars. They also have a child's menu. One location is in the basement of the Fine Arts Museum (the new building); other locations include 3200 Kirby Dr. (near the Village), 1422 West Gray (in the River Oaks shopping center), and 1101 Uptown Park (just off Post Oak in the Uptown area).

exclusively through donations by the restaurant's many loyal, if misguided, patrons. But is it art? You decide.

A few things must be cleared up. First, the "#7" is misleading; there cannot be seven such places in all of creation. This is it. There are a couple of Pig Stands still surviving in Beaumont and one in San Antonio, but those are very different in character. Second, the "pig sandwich" is not what brings people here. Mostly they come for classic Texas roadhouse fare such as chicken-fried steak, any of the breakfasts, the burgers and shakes, and of course, to be transported by the "porcine revival" decor set off by flourishes of Formica, vinyl, and imitation wood paneling. The Pig Stand is actually just a bit northwest of downtown.

This Is It. 207 West Gray. ☎ **713/659-1608.** Reservations not accepted. Main courses $7. AE, DISC, MC, V. Mon–Sat 11am–8pm, Sun 11am–6pm; breakfast daily 6:30–10am. West Gray is a continuation of Gray, which crosses Main St. 1 block south of the freeway overpass by the bus station. The restaurant is near the intersection with Bagby. SOUL FOOD.

If you yearn for soul food plain and simple, make your way over to this little place just southwest of downtown. Chitlins, clove-scented yams, meatloaf, braised oxtails, and lots of greens are served cafeteria-style. Owner Craig Joseph's wall of fame, photos of celebrities who have visited the restaurant, and the work of African American artists adorn the walls of this popular establishment. Recently this neighborhood was blanketed with townhouses. It's part of the Fourth Ward, which includes Freedmen's town, where the newly liberated slaves built their houses shortly after the Civil War. According to local historians, it was one of the most prosperous black communities in the South.

Treebeards. 315 Travis St. ☎ **713/228-2622.** Reservations not accepted. Main courses $5.15–$7.50. AE, DC, MC, V. Mon–Fri 11am–2pm, Fri 5–9pm. CREOLE.

It would be hard to find a place that gives you better food for your money. This is why Treebeards restaurant on Old Market Square gets such a crowd of office workers for lunch. Beat the crowd by going late or early and you can enjoy red beans and rice, chicken and shrimp gumbo, jambalaya, good cornbread, and all the rest. Food is served cafeteria-style. Look for three more downtown locations: 1117 Texas Ave. (next to Christ Church Cathedral), 1100 Louisiana (in the tunnel), and at 700 Rusk, at the corner of Louisiana Street.

2 East End

MODERATE

Kim Son. 2001 Jefferson. ☎ **713/222-2461.** Reservations accepted for parties of 8 or more. Main courses $6–$15. AE, DC, DISC, MC, V. Daily 11am–midnight. Located in the small Chinese commercial center a block east of the Brown Convention Center and the elevated Tex. 59 Freeway. VIETNAMESE/CHINESE.

The menu is the most imposing part of this casual, highly regarded Vietnamese restaurant. Don't worry, though, because there are no poor choices among the 100 or so options. Enjoy finely prepared delicacies as well as the expected fare, like terrific spring rolls and lovely noodle dishes. (The pan-seared shrimp with jalapeños and onions proves a delightful combination.) The menu includes several vegetarian dishes. Look for the exotic fish pool at the entrance. The restaurant has another location at 300 Milam near the theater district (☎ 713/222-2790).

INEXPENSIVE

✪ **Fiesta Loma Linda.** 2111 Telephone Rd. ☎ **713/924-6074.** Reservations not accepted. Main courses $5–$10; lunch specials $5.50–$6.50. AE, CB, DC, DISC, MC, V. Daily 10am–10pm (until 11 on weekends). Located 6 blocks off the Gulf Freeway (I-45). Exit Telephone Rd. and turn north; it will be on your right. TEX-MEX.

I like my Tex-Mex restaurants to be homey, unpretentious places where you're not likely to run into the see-and-be-seen crowd. Of course, that was true of all Tex-Mex restaurants before the rise of the fajita, which became so popular that it eventually pulled Tex-Mex into the cultural orbit of the truly trendy. Fiesta Loma Linda brings to mind those simpler times with its unselfconscious decoration and furniture and its utter lack of anything approaching trendiness. It also has an old-time 1930s tortilla maker specially designed to make the old-fashioned puffy tortillas that you always used to get when ordering chile con queso. The things to order here are, of course, the chile con queso for an appetizer and the puffy beef tacos, the beef or cheese enchiladas with chile gravy, and the combination dinners.

3 South Main

MODERATE

Fred's Italian Corner Restaurant. 2278 W. Holcombe. ☎ **713/665-7506.** Reservations not accepted. Main courses $5.25–$12. AE, CB, DC, DISC, MC, V. Mon–Fri 11am–3pm and 5–9:30pm (10:30 on Fri); Sat 5–10:30pm. From South Main drive west on Holcombe. Fred's is in a shopping center on your right, facing toward Greenbriar St. SOUTHERN ITALIAN.

This is a rarity in Houston—a true neighborhood Italian restaurant. The seating is tightly packed in the dining room, but that's part of the nature of these neighborhood institutions. You can get a good thin-crust pizza (an uncommon variety is the Sicilian pizza with shrimp, parsley, and eggs), pasta in many sauces, and a great selection of entrees, such as eggplant rollatini and the spinach tortellini clam Alfredo. The lunch specials are a good bargain—you order at the counter. The wine selection is fairly large and not overpriced.

INEXPENSIVE

Butera's. 4621 Montrose Blvd. ☎ **713/523-0722.** Salads $2.25–$8; soups $2–$6; sandwiches $6. AE, CB, DC, DISC, MC, V. Daily 11am–9pm. Located in Chelsea Market, a small mall on Montrose south of Bissonnet and just north of the freeway overpass. DELI.

A favorite haunt for museum-goers, this deli offers healthful fare in an airy and cheerful setting. Popular favorites include the Reuben sandwich, the Cobb salad, and the fettuccine Alfredo. Among the soups, the seafood gumbo is awfully good.

4 Montrose

VERY EXPENSIVE

⭐ **Mark's.** 1658 Westheimer. ☎ **713/523-3800.** Reservations recommended. Main courses $15–$26. AE, CB, DC, DISC, MC, V. Mon–Fri 11am–2pm; Mon–Thurs 6–11pm; Fri–Sat 5:30pm–midnight; Sun 5–10pm. NEW AMERICAN.

Many in Houston believe this to be the city's best restaurant, and they won't get any quarrel from this reviewer. Mark Cox, the former chef at Tony's, has a good idea of the direction in which American cooking should be headed—fresh ingredients prepared in a manner that's new and creative while being hearty and satisfying. There is a set menu that changes seasonally and a menu of daily specials, but a representative sampling of dishes would include grilled shrimp on a bed of fennel, basil, and tomato with a crab risotto, bourbon-glazed pork with yams and an apple compote, roasted breast of chicken with Mississippi-style grits scented with white truffles, or lamb in a basil sauce with white cheddar potatoes. The restaurant occupies an abandoned church on Westheimer. The main dining room is in the nave, and a small dining area is in the choir loft. Alongside the nave, the owners have built an eye-catching, smaller dining room with Gothic rib vaulting.

EXPENSIVE

Backstreet Café. 1103 S. Shepherd. ☎ **713/521-2239.** Reservations recommended. Main courses $13–$19. AE, MC, V. Sun–Thurs 11am–10pm; Fri–Sat 11am–11pm. Despite the address, the restaurant is located a block east of Shepherd and 2 blocks north of West Gray and the River Oaks Shopping Center, off McDuffie St. NEW AMERICAN.

Wonderful cooking, a good selection of wines, and excellent service make this place perennially popular. All the starters are delicious creations, including the portobello mushrooms stuffed with shrimp and crawfish, pot stickers with shrimp and shiitake mushrooms, and smoked corn crab cakes. Main courses include many dishes with crusts, such as pepper crusted pork tenderloin, potato crusted red snapper (very good), and mustard crusted salmon. This puts the chefs at some risk of being criticized as trendy, but they were cooking these dishes long before putting crusts on things became so popular. For those who rebel against this trend, there are dishes such as the meatloaf tower with mushroom gravy and garlic mashed potatoes on the side—an excellent combination of new and old tastes. All the entrees come accompanied by side dishes such as corn pudding or potato pancakes. Dining areas include two upstairs rooms, one downstairs room, and a lovely patio shaded by trees. Don't even try to park your car; let the valet do it.

MODERATE

Baba Yega. 2607 Grant St. ☎ **713/522-0042.** Reservations not accepted. Main courses $10–$14; sandwiches $6–$9. AE, DC, DISC, MC, V. Mon–Thurs 11am–10pm; Fri–Sat 11am–11pm; Sun 11am–10pm. Located 2 blocks north of Westheimer (turn at the Felix Mexican Restaurant) and 2 blocks east of Montrose Blvd. SANDWICHES/PASTA/VEGETARIAN.

Set in a small bungalow on a side street off Westheimer, Baba Yega is one of the hippest places in the Montrose. The restaurant offers several small dining areas, all of which are agreeable, particularly the garden veranda in back. Next door is an herb shop that belongs to the owner, and, whenever possible, he cooks with his own herbs. The most popular lunch items are the sandwiches, of which there are several vegetarian choices. For dinner, the daily specials are what most people order, and these usually include at least one chicken and one fish dish. Tuesday is the "Italian Special," a plate of pasta and glass of wine. A particularly good entree is the chicken *pomodoro*.

La Mexicana Restaurant. 1018 Fairview. ☎ **713/521-0963.** Reservations not accepted. Main courses $7–$13. AE, DC, DISC, MC, V. Daily 7am–11pm. Located on the corner of Montrose and Fairview (first traffic light north of Westheimer). MEXICAN.

Once a little Mexican grocery store, La Mexicana started serving tacos and gradually turned exclusively to the restaurant business. It's well known for delicious Mexican breakfasts such as *huevos a la Mexicana* or *migas* (both particularly good, as are their frijoles and the green *salsa de mesa*), and classic enchilada plates (red or green are good choices). Some dishes are "muy auténtico," such as the *nopalitos en salsa chipotle* or the tacos *de guisado de puerco* or *de chicharrón en salsa verde* (one of my favorites, but not for everyone). Other dishes are Tex-Mex standbys, such as the fajitas and the combination plates. Service is good, and there's a choice of outside or inside dining.

5 Kirby District

EXPENSIVE

✪ **Churrascos.** 2055 Westheimer. ☎ **713/527-8300.** Reservations recommended. Main courses $14–$24; lunch $7.50–$9.50. AE, CB, DC, DISC, MC, V. Mon–Thurs 11am–10pm; Fri 11am–11pm; Sat 5–11pm. SOUTH AMERICAN/ STEAKS.

When this restaurant opened about 10 years ago, it caught on like a house on fire. The owners have since opened another restaurant, Américas (see review below). This has thinned the crowds somewhat, and fans of this place couldn't be happier. This is simpler and more elegant than Américas, and a good bit less noisy. It is modeled after a simple Argentinean estancia in colors of white, red, and black. The signature dish is the butterflied beef tenderloin served with *chimichurri* sauce, the Argentine condiment that always accompanies steak. Also very different for the Houston dining scene are the fried plantain chips served at every table, the Argentinean empanadas, the Cuban-style black bean soup, and the Peruvian-style ceviche. Grilled vegetables are served "family style" with every entree. All in all, the menu is less "out there" and less trendy than Américas, but it can't be considered humdrum. For dessert, the restaurant is famous for its *tres leches* cake, and justifiably so.

MODERATE

Goode Company Texas Barbecue. 5109 Kirby Dr. ☎ **713/522-2530.** Barbecue plates $7–$10. AE, DC, DISC, MC, V. Daily 11am–10pm. BARBECUE.

Jim Goode, a local name in the restaurant business, cooks up some great barbecue at this rickety joint on Kirby, 4 blocks south of the Southwest Freeway. Beer signs and country music on the jukebox set the scene. To get great smoked flavor, Mr. Goode cooks with the greenest wood he can find. Especially tasty are the pork ribs and the brisket, but you can also get duck, chicken, and links. Order by the pound, the plate, or the sandwich. For dessert, the pecan pie is a must. There is an additional location in west Houston at 8911 Katy Freeway (☎ **713/464-1901**).

Jalapeños. 2702 Kirby Dr. ☎ **713/524-1668.** Main courses $9–$17. AE, DC, DISC, MC, V. Mon–Thurs 11am–10pm; Fri–Sat 11am–11pm; Sun 10:30am–10pm (Sun brunch until 2:30pm). MEXICAN/TEX-MEX.

In Houston, Mexican food restaurants run the gamut from basic fajitas, to classic *alta cocina,* to new wave *nueva cocina;* this restaurant does a good job of crossing genres to create a menu with plenty of variety. You can get fajitas for sure (prepared with a lovely marinade and grilled over an honest wood fire), but you can also get spinach enchiladas, or fish cooked in the most popular Mexican versions—*al mojo de ajo* and *a la veracruzana.* The menu has several vegetarian options; the appetizers are good here and so is the black bean soup. They also have a long list of brand-name margaritas to try, though the house margarita isn't too shabby. The dining area isn't terribly large, but the big windows make it seem roomier and the bright colors make it a cheerful place. At times it can be a little noisy.

Lucinda's. 2415 Dunstan. ☎ **713/394-7280.** Main courses $8–$17; lunch specials $5.95. AE, DC, DISC, MC, V. Tues–Thurs 11am–10pm; Fri–Sat 11am–11pm; Sun 11am–10pm. Located in the northeastern corner of Rice Village, 4 blocks off Kirby, near the intersection with Morningside. TEX-MEX.

Lucinda's is just what western civilization needs—a family restaurant that serves an excellent and generous margarita. The large dining room has modern and playful décor with a riot of colors and fans suspended from a high ceiling. Off to one side is an enclosed game room for the kids who don't want to stay at the table. The crowd is usually a mix of young professionals and families. A bar area accommodates those wanting only drinks. The most popular items on the menu are from the grill. If you are feeling particularly hungry or have a lot of mouths to feed, try the *parrillada* for two; it's a large offering of different grilled specialties including shrimp, quail, fajitas, and *carnitas.* For the less ambitious, there's always a taco *al carbón* plate (they make their own flour tortillas here). Portions are generous. There are a couple of vegetarian items on the menu, but vegetarians can do better elsewhere.

ℹ Family-Friendly Restaurants

Lucinda's *(see p. 67)*   With its fun Tex-Mex menu, good margaritas for the parents, and an enclosed game room for the
young and the restless, Lucinda's is immensely popular with
families.

Pig Stand #7 *(see p. 60)*   Children enjoy all the various and
sundry representations of pigs here, as well as the menu of burgers and shakes. The jukebox, with its repertoire of country-
and-western classics, also grabs their attention.

James Coney Island *(see p. 60)*   What hot dog place isn't popular with kids? But most of these restaurants are decorated in
bright colors that make them especially attractive to the young,
and they offer kid's specials.

✪ **Thai Spice.** 5117 Kelvin. ☎ **713/522-5100.** Main courses $8.50–$11;
lunch buffet $7.95. AE, DC, DISC, MC, V. Mon–Sat 11am–2:30pm (lunch buf-
fet); and 5–10pm; Sun 11:30am–3pm, 5–9pm. Located a couple of blocks east
of Kirby at the corner of Kelvin and Dunstan, by an Antone's food market. THAI.

Houston is particularly rich in Thai restaurants, and, in the
Rice Village, there are three highly recommended ones, each
with its own loyal following. Of these, Thai Spice gets the
nod; mostly because the service is friendlier and the dining
area is roomier, more attractive, and better furnished, but also
because the food is a particularly appealing interpretation of
Thai that doesn't burn out your taste buds. The lunch buffet
is worthy of special note for offering better variety and quality
than in most places. The dinner menu is well laid out and
doesn't try to confuse you with options by listing the same
basic dish four times. The spicy shrimp soup is good, and the
"summer palace" is a great spicy option for a stir-fry. There are
also several mild dishes, including a wonderfully simple grilled
lemongrass chicken breast. All of the curries are worth ordering, and the pad Thai is excellent.

INEXPENSIVE

Luling City Market. 4726 Richmond Ave. ☎ **713/871-1903.** Reservations
not accepted. Barbecue plates $6.70–$8.50. AE, DC, DISC, MC, V. Mon–Sat
11am–9pm; Sun noon–7pm. BARBECUE.

This is great barbecue served in a traditional setting, which for
Texas barbecue joints means that any effort spent decorating

appears, at least, as purely an afterthought and, at most, as the owner's misguided attempt to find a place for all the objets d'art that have been cluttering up his attic. This place follows the minimalist approach. Service is lunch counter style. I heartily recommend the ribs and the sausage. At night, the quiet little bar fills up with regulars with whom you can have some good-natured conversation, mostly about sports.

6   Uptown

VERY EXPENSIVE

Américas. 1800 Post Oak Blvd. ☎ **713/961-1492.** Reservations recommended. Main courses $15–$30. AE, CB, DC, DISC, MC, V. Mon–Thurs 11am–10pm; Fri 11am–11pm; Sat 5–11pm. PAN-AMERICAN.

Stuck in a gastronomical rut? This restaurant is an admirable choice for busting loose. From the way-out décor that combines realistic representations of Incan stonework, blown-up images of Indian basketry, and a polychromatic rain forest canopy, to the highly inventive menu of dishes loosely inspired by the national cuisines of the New World, there is nothing ho-hum about dining here. Corn-crusted gulf red snapper with a Mexican cream sauce, the yucca polenta, and a refined version of *anticuchos* (a favorite street food in Peru) are indicative of what you can order. Wildly popular with Houston natives, the restaurant is packed most nights; make sure to get reservations for dining, or perhaps stop by for drinks and a glance at the brave new surroundings. My biggest complaint about the restaurant is the noise level.

MODERATE

Sammy's Lebanese Restaurant. 5825 Richmond. ☎ **713/780-0065.** Reservations only for 6 or more. Main courses $9–$14. AE, CB, DC, DISC, MC, V. Mon–Thurs 11am–10:30pm; Fri–Sat 11am–11pm; Sun noon–10pm. LEBANESE.

While there are more elaborate and upscale Middle Eastern options in town, this very casual and friendly restaurant remains a longtime favorite for its mouth-watering, inexpensive food and a surprising wine list. It's popular for its appetizer platters, and offers a large selection of seafood and vegetarian dishes. Baked kibbe, sure, but check out the chicken wings and garlic-laced mashed-potato dip. Sammy's is on a stretch of Richmond Avenue just a few blocks west of the Uptown area, known as the "Richmond Strip" for its many clubs and restaurants.

7 Far West Houston

VERY EXPENSIVE

Lynn's Steakhouse. 955 Dairy Ashford. ☎ **281/870-0807.** Reservations recommended. Steaks $28–$37. AE, CB, DC, EC, MC, V. Mon–Fri 10am–2pm and 5–10pm; Sat 5–10pm. From downtown, take the Katy Freeway (I-10 west). Look for Dairy Ashford, which is the second exit after the Sam Houston Parkway. STEAKS.

This restaurant in far west Houston is a favorite steakhouse for those who can afford it and who like a bottle of wine to accompany their steak. It is especially known for its melt-in-your-mouth fillets and chateaubriand and for its extensive wine list that wins high praise from grape enthusiasts. Salads come with every steak, and vegetables are a la carte. The bread is homemade. The dining rooms are comfortable and quiet with ample space between tables, and reservations truly mean something here. The dress code precludes shorts or T-shirts.

6

What to See & Do in Houston

S ince Houston isn't generally considered a major tourist destination, there isn't much in the way of tourism infrastructure except for the downtown visitor's center. Most of the available resources are geared towards conventions and large groups, not independent travelers. This means that you'll have to work harder to find information about the city's attractions. A case-in-point is downtown Houston, which has fascinating and important architecture by internationally prominent architects and a lot of public sculpture and art works by important sculptors and painters; yet, there is no regularly scheduled tour of downtown. If you're interested in finding a tour of downtown, see "Organized Tours," later in this chapter; the following listings, organized geographically, will guide you to Houston's many points of interest.

1 The Top Attractions

DOWNTOWN

Heritage Society at Sam Houston Park. 1100 Bagby. ☎ **713/655-1912.**
Tours $6 adults, $4 seniors and children ages 13–17, $2 children 6–12, free for children under 6. Mon–Sat 10am–3pm; Sun 1–3pm.

Just a couple of blocks from Houston's visitor's center is this park that serves as a repository for eight of Houston's oldest houses and buildings, that were transferred here from their original locations. The oldest building dates prior to Texas's Independence; it is a small and simple cabin originally built close to where NASA is today. A freed slave built another house in 1870, and there's a church dating from 1892. The Heritage Society has worked hard to restore them to their original state and furnish them with pieces from the appropriate era. The only way to see these buildings is by guided tour, which leaves every hour on the hour from the tour office at 1100 Bagby. The guides are well informed and add a lot to a visit here. The Heritage Museum can be visited without taking the tour. It features permanent exhibits of Texas history.

Downtown tunnel system. Accessible through any building connected to the tunnel system. Free admission. Mon–Fri 7am–6pm.

There are 6 miles of tunnels below Houston's downtown, most of them private property. Along those corridors are food courts, restaurants, shops, and businesses of all varieties. You can get a map of the tunnels from the city's visitor's center, or you can take a guided tour if you schedule it in advance. See "Organized Tours," later in this section.

EAST END & BEYOND

✪ **The Orange Show.** 2401 Munger St. ☎ **713/926-6368.** www.orangeshow.org. Admission $1 adults, free for children under 12. Open Memorial Day to Labor Day Wed–Fri 9am–1pm, Sat–Sun noon–5pm; mid-Mar–mid-Dec Sat–Sun noon–5pm. From downtown, take Gulf Fwy. Take the Telephone Rd. exit and make the third right off the feeder road on to Munger (before you get to the Telephone Rd. intersection).

This may not be the "greatest show on earth," but it sure is the quirkiest. In truth, it's not a show at all, at least not as we commonly understand the word *show*. Rather, it's the life work of one man, former postman Jeff McKissack, who spent his last 25 years assembling a collection of found objects and building materials into an architectural collage that students of folk art call a "folk art environment." It stands in a quiet working-class neighborhood just off the Gulf Freeway, where it dares to be different. With its many flagpoles, spindles, wagon wheels, and wrought iron birds rising up from behind its walls, it seems like an outpost for spontaneity in a wilderness of cookie-cutter ranch-style houses.

Inside, the viewer is presented with all kinds of curiosities: two small arenas, observation decks, a small museum, and lots of cheerful wrought iron decoration and tile work. Inscriptions adorn the walls; many of these honor that best of all fruits, "The orange: a great gift to mankind." Upon the death of Mr. McKissack, The Orange Show fell into decay until it was rescued by the Orange Show Foundation, located in the house across the street and a center for Houston's folk art world. It is the organizer of the Art Car Parade and the Art Car Ball (see "Houston & the Gulf Coast Calendar of Events" in chapter 2). It is also the organizer of Eyeopener Tours (see "Organized Tours," below). If you like folk art, consider purchasing their driving tour audiocassette of Houston's folk art treasures (the tape comes with a map).

Houston Ship Channel. 7300 Clinton Dr. at Gate 8. ☎ **713/670-2416.** Free admission. Tues–Sun 10am and 2:30pm; no morning trips Sun or Thurs. Call for reservations. Closed Sept and holidays. Take the Gulf Fwy. South; get on Loop 610 east, which takes you over the ship channel; exit Clinton Dr. Turn right on Clinton (look for small green signs pointing the way); after a mile, you'll come to a traffic light and a sign reading PORT GATE 8. Turn left.

For those fortunate enough not to live among the industrial areas along the Texas Gulf Coast, the landscape of refineries and their intricate tangle of pipes, their forests of cooling towers and stacks, and their fields of tanks are as exotic as the Zanzibar coast. If you find this sort of thing intriguing, you can take a free boat ride on the Sam Houston Inspection Ship, which tours the upper 7 miles of the deep-water channel. The boat dates from the 1950s and has a lovely cabin trimmed in mahogany and fore and aft decks for observation. You should probably make reservations for the boat ride well in advance during the summer months when it's quite popular, however, I'm told that the ship channel is best seen in cooler weather, when there's no risk of bad smells. The trip takes a total of 90 minutes, during which you will most likely see large container ships, tall grain elevators, and tugs and barges. If after the trip, you want to see more of the channel, you can drive to the San Jacinto Battlefield, where the Battleship *Texas* is on display (see review below).

Battleship *Texas* and San Jacinto Monument and Museum. 3527 Battleground Rd. ☎ **281/479-2431.** Battleship admission $5 adults, $4 seniors, $3 children ages 6–18, free for children under 6; monument and museum admission is free; observation room $3 adults, $2 children age 11 and under; movie $3.50 adults, $2.50 children age 11 and under. Daily 10am–5pm. Take the La Porte Fwy. (Tex. 225) east from Loop 610 east. For 15 miles you will pass large refineries and tank farms. (If tears well up in your eyes and your throat muscles begin to constrict involuntarily, you'll know you're headed in the right direction.) Exit Battleground Rd. (Tex.134) and turn left.

On the San Jacinto Battleground in 1836, Texas won its independence from Mexico with a crushing surprise attack by the Texas forces, whose battle cry was "Remember the Alamo!" To commemorate that victory, civic leaders in 1936 built a

Central Houston Attractions

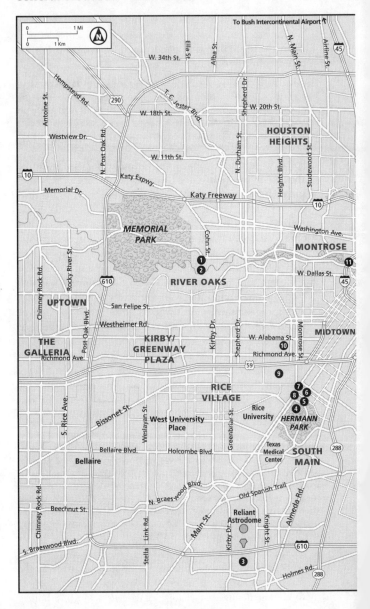

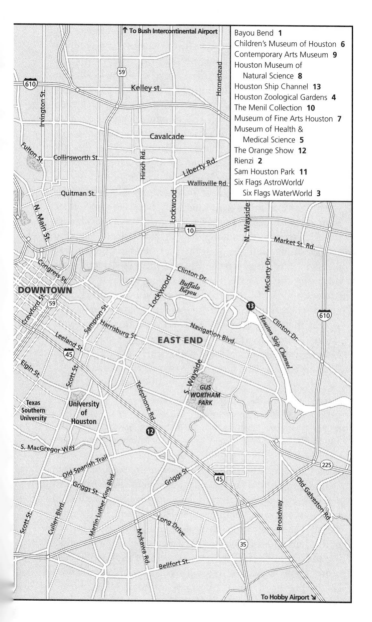

↑ To Bush Intercontinental Airport

Bayou Bend **1**
Children's Museum of Houston **6**
Contemporary Arts Museum **9**
Houston Museum of
    Natural Science **8**
Houston Ship Channel **13**
Houston Zoological Gardens **4**
The Menil Collection **10**
Museum of Fine Arts Houston **7**
Museum of Health &
    Medical Science **5**
The Orange Show **12**
Rienzi **2**
Sam Houston Park **11**
Six Flags AstroWorld/
    Six Flags WaterWorld **3**

610

59

Kelley st.

Homestead

Irvington St.

Fulton St.

Collinsworth St.

Cavalcade

Hirsch Rd.

Liberty Rd.

Quitman St.

Wallisville Rd.

Lockwood

N. Main St.

10

N. Wayside

Market St. Rd.

McCarty Dr.

Congress St.

Clinton Dr.

Buffalo
Bayou

Lockwood

DOWNTOWN

59

Crawford St.

Sampson St.

Harrisburg St.

Navigation Blvd.

EAST END

Clinton Dr.

610

Houston Ship Channel

13

Leeland St.

45

Elgin St.

Scott St.

S. Wayside

**GUS
WORTHAM
PARK**

Texas
Southern
University

**University
of
Houston**

Telephone Rd.

12

S. MacGregor Way

Old Spanish Trail

225

Griggs St.

45

Scott St.

Cullen Blvd.

Martin Luther King Blvd.

Griggs St.

Old Galveston Rd.

Broadway

Mykawa Rd.

Long Drive

35

Bellfort St.

To Hobby Airport ↘

towering obelisk as tall as the Washington Monument but topped with a Texas Lone Star. In the base of the monument is a small museum of Texas history with some interesting exhibits, such as one about the relatively unsung Texas hero "Deaf" Smith, and a collection of watercolors of the Mexican War painted by Sam Chamberlain. There is also a small auditorium where you can watch a 35-minute documentary of the battle. If you would like to view some of the Port of Houston as well as the rest of the land for miles around, you can take the elevator up to the observation room in the top floor of the tower, which is more than 500 feet above the ground.

Across from the monument, in roughly the same place from where the Texas forces began their advance, is the USS *Texas*. Built in 1914, before improvements in warplane technology made these large dreadnought battleships vulnerable, she is the last of her kind. Between the wars, the navy modernized the ship with antiaircraft and torpedo defenses, but it's still surprising that it survived the war, having fought in both the Atlantic and Pacific theaters. When you visit you can clamber up to its small-caliber guns or onto the navigation bridge, inspect the crew's quarters and check out the engine room. Life on board was no picnic—the quarters were cramped and facilities were minimal—so it's interesting to note that this ship was considered a lucky assignment.

✪ **Space Center Houston.** 1601 NASA Rd. 1, Clear Lake. ☎ **281/ 244-2100.** Admission (including tours and IMAX theater) $14.95 adults, $13.95 seniors, $10.95 children ages 4–11, free for children 3 and under. Daily 9am–7pm in summer; otherwise Mon–Fri 10am–5pm, Sat–Sun 10am–7pm. Parking $3. The Space Center is about 25 miles from downtown Houston. Take the Gulf Fwy. to NASA Rd. 1, turn left, and go 3 miles.

Space Center Houston is the visitor's center for NASA's Johnson Space Center, and it's the product of the joint efforts by NASA and Disney Imagineering. It's the most popular attraction in Houston, and there's nothing quite like it anywhere else in the world. There are plenty of exhibits and activities to interest both adults and children, and they do a great job of introducing the visitor to different aspects of space exploration. The center banks heavily on interactive displays and simulations on the one hand and actual access to the real thing on the other. For instance, the Feel of Space gallery simulates working in the frictionless environment of space by using an air-bearing floor (something like a giant air hockey table). Another simulator shows what it's like to land the lunar orbiter. For a direct experience of NASA, you can take the 1½-hour tram tour that takes you, among other places, to the International Space Station Assembly Building and NASA control center. You get to see things as they happen, especially interesting if there's a shuttle mission in progress. You might also see astronauts in training. And, on top of all this, Space Center Houston has the largest IMAX in Texas.

Kemah Boardwalk. Tex. 146, Kemah. ☎ **877/285-3624.**

Many visitors to NASA will go out for seafood afterward at nearby Kemah, which is as touristy as the Houston area gets. It used to be a rustic shrimping port on Galveston Bay where you could buy some shrimp and a beer and sit by the dock on an afternoon to watch the shrimp boats come in. Most of the pier was blown away in 1984 by a hurricane, and in the 1990s, a developer bought it and built a boardwalk, several restaurants, a hotel, and some touristy stores and attractions. The restaurants overlook the water; if you stroll down the boardwalk, you'll pass every one. Pick the one that appeals most to you. Among the attractions is a 50,000-gallon, floor-to-ceiling aquarium housing more than 100 species of tropical fish in the Aquarium Restaurant.

SOUTH MAIN/MUSEUM DISTRICT

Museum of Fine Arts, Houston (MFAH). 1001 Bissonnet St. ☎ **713/639-7300.** www.mfah.org. $5 adults, $2.50 seniors and children ages 6–18, free for children 5 and under; free general admission every Thurs. Tues, Wed, and Sat 10am–7pm; Thurs–Fri 10am–9pm; Sun 12:15–7pm.

This is, by far, the best and biggest public art museum in Texas. It's a wonderful testament to what a lot of oil money can do, and the manner in which it evolved tells something about the development of the city's sense of aesthetics. The original museum, built in the 1920s, was pure neoclassical— the attitude was that if Houston was to have a museum, it was to look like a museum. In the '50s, the MFAH directors hired Mies van der Rohe, the grand architect of the International Style to build an addition. In the '70s, that addition received an addition, also designed by Mies. Both of these were bold statements of modern architecture—lots of glass and steel forming a light and airy space—but, unfortunately, not the kind of space that lends itself well for the exhibition of much of the museum's collection. Because the additions were so large, the museum found itself with a disproportionate amount of open exhibition space.

In the '90s, the museum's directors hired Spanish architect Rafael Moneo to design a building that would be a return to traditional galleries. It, the **Audrey Jones Beck Building,** opened last year on South Main Street across from the main building. (A tunnel connects the two; make a point of visiting it.) The new building aims at reconciling the boldness of modernism with the staid character of traditional design, thereby creating a kind of new traditionalism. Constructed with rich materials and designed on grand proportions, the building feels monumental to the visitor. All the galleries on the second floor take advantage of interesting "roof lanterns" that allow Houston's plentiful natural light to enter in regulated amounts. The Beck building doubles MFAH's gallery space and allows the directors to attract first-rate traveling exhibitions. The museum's collection of more than 40,000 pieces is wide and varied, but it is perhaps strongest in the area of impressionist and postimpressionist works, baroque and Renaissance art, and 19th- and 20th-century American art. There's also a fine collection of African tribal art, as well as ancient artwork from several civilizations.

Aside from the two gallery buildings, there is a large **sculpture garden** designed by Isamu Noguchi located across Bissonnet from the main building, and the **Glassell School of Art,** which can be seen just to the north of the sculpture garden. Look for a building made of a strangely reflective glass brick (another architectural pun). The museum also owns two collections of the decorative arts that are displayed in two mansions in the River Oaks Area; see **Bayou Bend** and **Rienzi** in the section on attractions in the Kirby District, below.

Contemporary Arts Museum. 5216 Montrose Blvd. ☎ **713/284-8250.** www.camh.org. Free admission. Tues–Sat 10am–5pm, Thurs until 9pm; Sun noon–5pm.

This silver-aluminum parallelogram, located on the corner of Montrose and Bissonnet, cater-corner to the Fine Arts Museum, presents temporary exhibitions of modern art and design. It has no permanent collection; what you might find here is purely the luck of the draw.

Children's Museum of Houston. 1500 Binz. ☎ **713/522-1138.** www. cmhouston.com. $5 per person; children under 2 are free; free family night Thurs 5–8pm. Tues–Sat 9am–5pm; Sun noon–5pm; also Mon 9am–5pm Memorial Day to Labor Day only.

The goal behind the Children's Museum was to create a place where children can engage the world around them on their own terms, a place that will spark their imaginations, and a place where they will learn the joy of discovery. It's for children up to 12 years old, but even if you're without kids in tow, you might like to take a glance at the museum's fun exterior, designed by Robert Venturi in association with Jackson & Ryan Architects of Houston. It's a playful send-up of the classical museum facade and is apt clothing for this institution that blurs the distinction between museum and playhouse.

It's obvious that the museum's staff is very much in touch with their inner child. They have developed such fun, interactive exhibits as Bubble Lab and Kid-TV, which gives kids the opportunity to imitate what they see on the tube while giving them a behind-the-scenes understanding of television production. Another exhibit recreates the Mexican Indian village of Yalalag; another, called Tot Spot, focuses on the 6-month to 3-year-old crowd, helping build motor skills through ingenious forms of play. The museum managers bring in many visitors and special shows; it would be wise to inquire about what they might be planning to do during your visit. The Children's Museum is on the same street as the MFAH (the street name changes from Bissonnet to Binz), 4 blocks to the east. The best time to go is in the afternoon when there is less probability of school trip crowds.

Museum of Health & Medical Science. 1515 Hermann Dr. ☎ **713/521-1515.** www.mhms.org. Admission $4 adults, $3 children ages 4–12, $2 seniors, free for children 3 and under; free admission on "Free Family Thursdays" 4–7pm. Tues–Sat 9am–5pm; Sun noon–5pm.

We have all heard about just what an amazing thing the human body is, but just how well are most of us really acquainted with its workings? This family museum will surprise most visitors with its extensive use of audio, video, holograms, and medical technology to provide a graphic view of human physiology. Because of the Texas Medical Center, Houston has a large medical community, which has been the driving force behind the creation of this museum. With additional contributions from corporations and individual doctors, it has constructed an eye-catching interactive exhibition called the **Amazing Body Pavilion.** The exhibit is itself a metaphor for the body. Visitors enter through the mouth and proceed down the digestive tract learning about all the organs that process our food. (Children seem to think this is pretty cool.) The exhibit covers all the major organs in ways that provide lots of interaction for children, and explanatory text and monologues by little holographic figures are well written and manage to provide info that most adults will find interesting. Of course, with so many doctors involved, you can be sure that there will be some preaching about the need for a good diet and to avoid smoking, and don't expect the museum's snack bar to offer any junk food. But do check out the gift shop; it has an assortment of curious and intriguing items that you won't easily find elsewhere. One other note: You might want to ask at the front desk about the next scheduled organ dissection. When I was there, the organ of the month was the sheep brain; I opted to forego the performance. The museum is 1 block south of the Children's Museum.

Houston Museum of Natural Science. 1 Hermann Circle Dr. ☎ 713/ 639-4629. www.hmns.org. General admission $5 adults, $3 seniors and children ages 3–11, free for children age 2 and under; planetarium and Butterfly Center each are $4 adults, $3 seniors and children ages 3–11, free for children age 2 and under; IMAX tickets $6.50 adults, $4.50 seniors and children ages 3–11, free for children age 2 and under. Multi-venue ticket packages available. General hours Mon–Sat 9am–6pm, Sun 11am–6pm; hours for Butterfly Center and IMAX can differ. Parking $3; garage entrance on Caroline St.

This is all a natural science museum should be and then some. In the museum proper you can find dinosaur skeletons, displays of Texas wildlife, a stunning gem and mineral collection, a Foucault pendulum, and exhibits on early cultures of the Americas, climatology, chemistry, and oil and gas exploration and production. But what gets most of the buzz is the miniature rain forest environment, created in the Butterfly Center. You can walk among hundreds of living butterflies as they dance about in the steamy air amidst a small waterfall. As you enter, you pass through the insect zoo, which holds some fascinating and bizarre living specimens of beetles, spiders, and other bugs that you wouldn't necessarily want running around freely with you. Also in the museum are an IMAX theater and

It's in the Air

Houston has earned the unofficial nickname of "Air Conditioning Capital of the World." In the summer, the air can be hot and uncommonly humid. If you are unaccustomed to high humidity, allow a day to let your body adjust, drink plenty of water, and plan indoor activities. Many visitors experience languor and sluggishness at first, but this will dissipate with time.

a planetarium. The museum recently reequipped the planetarium with new computer animation projectors that enhance the visual quality of its programs about stars, galaxies, nebulas, and other astral bodies. One more thing of note about this museum is that in years past, the directors have assembled some great temporary exhibits, so ask about any temporary shows that might be open during your visit. The museum occupies a corner of the Hermann Park about 3 blocks from the Fine Arts Museum next to the equestrian statue of Sam Houston.

Hermann Park. Fannin St. at Hermann Park Dr.

This park has 545 acres of land and lies just beyond the Museum District and west of South Main Street. The parkland is well wooded and has an 18-hole public golf course, picnic areas, and playscapes. Near the Natural Science Museum, which borders the park, is a Garden Center with beautiful rose gardens and a garden of aromatic herbs. Also in that vicinity is a Japanese garden and Miller Outdoor Theater, which often holds free plays and musical performances.

Houston Zoological Gardens. 1513 N. MacGregor. ☎ **713/523-5888.** Daily 10am–6pm. $2.50 adults, $2 seniors, 50¢ children ages 3–12, free for children age 2 and under.

Located within Hermann Park is this 50-acre zoo featuring a gorilla habitat, rare albino reptiles, cat facility, huge aquarium, and vampire bats that eat lunch every day at 2:30pm. The Brown Education Center, open daily from 10am to 6pm, allows visitors to interact with the animals.

Six Flags AstroWorld & Six Flags WaterWorld. 9001 Kirby Dr. ☎ **713/ 799-1234.** www.sixflags.com. AstroWorld $36 adults, $25 seniors 55 and older, $18 children under 48 in., free for children under age 3. WaterWorld $20 adults, $15 children under 48 in., $14 seniors 55 and older, free for children under age 3. Prices do not include tax. AstroWorld is generally open daily late May to late Aug, Fri–Sun Mar–May and Sept–Nov; closed Nov–Feb. Hours generally 11am–10pm, depending on the season. WaterWorld is open only during the summer months. Call ahead or check the website, since times often vary. Parking $5.

Farther south of Hermann Park and the Texas Medical Center is the Astrodome, and just south of it, across the Loop 610 Freeway, are these two large amusement parks. AstroWorld is a 75-acre park with several high-tech roller coasters, other thrill rides, performance venues, and theme areas. Highlights include the Serial Thriller, a roller coaster that has you suspended in a seat while it twirls you through seven inversions. In Dungeon Drop, you can experience free-fall, and the Texas Tornado steel roller coaster does four loops at breakneck speed. Almost all of these rides are for children 48 inches or taller. For smaller children, there are themed areas such as the one based on Warner Bros. Looney Tunes characters. Water-World is one of those aquatic amusement parks that requires a sturdy bathing suit. It's full of water rides and games with a mixture of chutes and slides that you ride with or without a raft or other device. Again, many require that children be 48 inches or taller. The entrance to WaterWorld is next to that of AstroWorld. Six Flags owns another, larger water park called SplashTown, located north of Houston in the town of Spring; see "Farther Afield," below.

MONTROSE

✪ **Menil Collection.** 1515 Sul Ross St. ☎ **713/525-9400.** www. menil. org. Free admission. Wed–Sun 11am–7pm.

Here, on display in a quiet, unremarkable neighborhood near the University of St. Thomas, is one of the world's great private collections. The collectors, Jean and Dominique de Menil, arrived in Houston in the 1940s after fleeing from the war in Europe. For more than 4 decades, they purchased and commissioned works of art. In addition, they brought artists, architects, and academics to the city, organized groundbreaking exhibitions, and did much for Houston's art museums and for the art departments of Rice University and St. Thomas University. Their collection, especially the modern art, is vast, so much so that only a fifth of it can be exhibited in the museum at one time. Renzo Piano, who worked closely with Mrs. de Menil, designed the building housing the collection. It is graceful and personable and doesn't seek to impress the visitor or impose itself on the collection. In these qualities, it is the physical embodiment of Mrs. de Menil's ideas about experiencing art. When you walk into the museum there is nothing between you and the art—no grand lobby with marble stairway, no large banners or gift shop vying for attention, no tickets to buy, no tape-recorded tours. Viewing the art becomes a direct and personal experience.

The Menil Collection is concentrated in four areas: antiquity; Byzantine and Medieval; tribal art; and 20th century. This may seem an incongruous mix, but, strangely enough, it holds together. The collectors never intended to gather up the best or most representative of a period; they simply followed their own tastes, which were modern. And one interesting consequence of this fact (intended or not) is that, in walking through these galleries one right after another, the viewer gradually discerns a universality in the form of expression of some modern art. This artistic expression connects all the way back to the aesthetics of antiquity and all the way across the boundaries of western culture to the tribal peoples of other continents.

In addition to the main museum, there are four satellite buildings to visit that form a museum campus of sorts. (The Menil Foundation also purchased all the houses around the museum and painted them the same shade of green gray as the museum itself.) One of these satellite buildings is the much-talked-about **Rothko Chapel,** with its 14 brooding paintings by Mark Rothko, created specifically for this installation and the last works by the artist before his death. In front of the chapel stands Barnett Newman's *Broken Obelisk.* A block south of the Rothko Chapel is the **Byzantine Fresco Chapel Museum,** which is worth the viewing, as much for the building that houses them (designed by François de Menil, son of Jean and Dominique) as for the frescoes themselves, which were ransomed from international art thieves. Across the street from the main museum, in a building also designed by Renzo Piano, is a permanent exhibition of the works of **Cy Twombly,** which, though perhaps difficult to approach, are easy to view owing to the gallery's exquisite light. It lends a luminous quality to the large artworks, and somehow just being in the place livens one's spirits. Finally, there is

Richmond Hall, 2 blocks south of the campus, which holds an installation by neon light artist Don Flavin.

KIRBY DISTRICT

✪ **Bayou Bend.** 1 Westcott St. ☎ **713/639-7750.** Admission $10 adults, $8.50 seniors, $5 youths ages 10–18. Tues–Fri 10am–5pm; Sat 10am–12:45pm. Reservations required. Children under age 10 admitted only Sat–Sun 1–5pm; no admission fee.

Ima Hogg was daughter of Gov. Jim Hogg, a man who obviously had a cruel sense of humor. Miss Hogg, however, did not grow up shy and self-effacing. Long after the governor was dead, she was a power to be reckoned with in local affairs and did much to keep the chicanery in city hall to a minimum. Houston's most prominent architect, John F. Staub, built her mansion, Bayou Bend, in the 1920s. It holds in its 28 rooms a treasure trove of American furniture, paintings, and decorative objects dating from colonial times to about 1870 and is set amid 14 acres of beautifully tended gardens in a variety of styles. This is a must-see for antiques collectors and gardeners. Part of the Museum of Fine Arts, the collection is shown by guided tour, for which you must make reservations. You can, however, see the gardens on your own. Bayou Bend is on the backside of River Oaks, but is unapproachable from the main entrance to the neighborhood. The only way to get there is to go down Memorial Drive, which follows the north shore of Buffalo Bayou, then turn left onto Westcott to enter the grounds.

Rienzi. 1406 Kirby Dr. ☎ **713/639-7800.** Admission $6 adults and children ages 12 and over, $4 seniors. Mon, Thurs–Sat 10am–4pm. Reservations required.

In a 1950s River Oaks mansion designed by John F. Staub, the Museum of Fine Arts displays its collection of European decorative arts. Most of the collection predates 1800. The family that lived here donated both the house and the collection. This museum will be of most interest to those who enjoy English porcelain or those curious about Houston's domestic architecture. Call for a tour.

FARTHER AFIELD

George Ranch Historical Park. 10215 FM 762, Richmond. ☎ **281/ 343-0218.** www.georgeranch.org. Admission $7.50 adults, $6.50 seniors 55 and over, $4 children ages 3–12, free for children age 2 and under. Daily 10am–5pm.

You can experience the life of four generations of a Texas family on this 400-acre outdoor museum, a working cattle ranch. Wander through a restored 1820s pioneer farm, an 1880s Victorian mansion, an 1890s cowboy encampment, and a 1930s ranch house. Savor Victorian-style tea on the porch of an 1890s mansion, or sit around the campfire with cowboys during a roundup and watch a crafts demonstration such as rope twisting. Picnic areas are provided. Take the Southwest Freeway (Tex. 59 south), before getting to the town of Richmond exit FM highway 762 and go 6 miles south.

SplashTown. Northbound I-45 at Louetts Rd., Spring. ☎ **281/355-3300.** www.sixflags.com. $23 adults; $16 children under 48 inches and seniors over 55. Daily 11am–10pm during summer months. Hours vary, call or check website. Follow I-45 north to Dallas; take Exit 69-A, before The Woodlands.

A 45-minute drive from downtown, SplashTown is larger and has a few more rides than WaterWorld. Special events are held, and live entertainment is offered throughout the season.

National Museum of Funeral History. 415 Barren Springs (north Houston, near airport). ☎ **281/876-3063.** www.nmfh.org/. $6 adults, $5 seniors over 54, $3 children ages 3–12, free for children under age 2. Mon–Sat 10am–4pm; Sun noon–4pm.

Do you give much thought to how you would like to be remembered once you've shuffled off this mortal coil? Or perhaps your thoughts just naturally drift toward things funereal? If so, then this private museum is the thing for you. Its owner, Service Corporation International, is the largest funeral company in the United States, and it has obviously taken pains to assemble the nation's largest collection of funeral memorabilia. The exhibits include a restored horse-drawn hearse, antique automobile hearses, and a 1916 Packard funeral bus. You can see memorabilia and trivia from the funerals of many famous people including Martin Luther King Jr., John Wayne, Elvis, Abraham Lincoln, JFK, Nixon, and many more. Other attractions include a full-size replica of King Tut's sarcophagus.

2 Especially for Kids

As a parent can quickly grasp, Houston is kid-friendly. Easily half of the above-mentioned attractions are geared for kids or have a large component especially suitable for them. A tour of southeast Houston will take you to **The Orange Show,** with which young kids display an almost instinctual connection; the boat trip on the **Ship Channel;** a visit to the **Battleship Texas;** and the wonders of **Space Center Houston.** After that, there's a visit to the boardwalk in **Kemah,** or a trip to the **beach** or to **Moody Gardens** in Galveston (see chapter 9). South of downtown, you have the Museum District, which includes the **Children's Museum,** the **Natural Science Museum,** and the **Health & Medical Science Museum** that captivate kids of various ages. The former has the Butterfly Center, the planetarium, and an IMAX theater; the latter has the Amazing Body Pavilion, which fascinated my test subject, a 5-year-old boy. And, of course, there's **Houston Zoological Gardens,** which has a children's zoo that specializes in the exploration of the different ecological zones of Texas. Further south are the theme parks **AstroWorld** and **WaterWorld,** which are very popular with kids 48 inches or taller, but most likely an exercise in frustration for those who aren't. To the north is **SplashTown,** another water park, and to the south- west is the **George Ranch Historical Park** for kids interested in cowboys and the Old West.

3 Organized Tours

If you'd like a bus tour of the city to help you get your bear- ings, you're out of luck. There are companies such as Gray Line, but they only offer tours to conventions and visiting groups, not the general public. There is, however, a different kind of tour offered to visitors that can go a long way to intro- ducing you to what makes Houston unique. If you're planning to be in Houston during the second weekend of the month, you might be able to sign up for one of the offbeat tours offered by **Eyeopener Tours.** Part of the Orange Show Foun- dation, they put together an occasional tour that focuses on a particularly interesting aspect of the city. Transportation by charter bus, snacks, and drinks are included in the price (usu- ally around $35). Past tours have included folk art sites of the city, places of worship, architectural highlights, architectural lowlights, blues centers, and ethnic markets. Most of those who participate are resident Houstonians who want to learn about an unknown part of the city. Eyeopener Tours also sells an audiocassette and map for a self-guided tour of Houston's folk art environments. This is a good offering if you're pretty good at following directions and working with a map. For information, call ☎ **713/926-6368** or check the website www.orangeshow.org/eyeopener.

The other option is walking tours (yes, walking tours in Houston) by **Houston Walks and the Houston Tunnel Association.** Sandra Lord, known locally as the Tunnel Lady, runs these walking tours. The tours are by appointment. One of the most popular is that of the Houston tunnel system, which includes several downtown sights. Other possible walking tours include the Museum District, and a tour of the public sculpture and art of downtown. Prices for tours vary. Ms. Lord occasionally offers scheduled seasonal walks that anyone can sign up for. You can contact her by e-mail at tunnellady@aol.com or call ☎ **713/222-9255.**

4 Outdoor & Spectator Sports

OUTDOOR SPORTS

BIKING, JOGGING & WALKING By far the most popular jogging and walking track is in **Memorial Park.** This is a large and beautiful park clothed in pine trees along Buffalo Bayou west of downtown, just inside the Loop. It's easy to reach; take Memorial Drive, which follows the north bank of Buffalo Bayou, from downtown to the park. It can be very crowded and doesn't work for biking, for which there are other trails. One biking option is to ride through **the Heights,** a quiet neighborhood of old houses and antiques shops not far from Memorial. Many visitors will prefer the hike and bike trail along the banks of **Buffalo Bayou** from North Shepherd to downtown. It offers lovely vistas of the downtown skyline and is decorated with numerous sculptures that can be both fun and interesting (and it takes you right into the Theater District). During the day it's fine, but I wouldn't advise venturing along the bayou at night. To rent a bike in this area, see **West End Cycles** at 5427 Blossom (☎ **713/225-6372**), which is in the neighborhood next to Memorial Park. They can set you up and give you information about good rides.

A longer hike and bike trail runs along the banks of **Brays Bayou** from Hermann Park through the Medical Center, where it goes under South Main Street then heads southwest almost all the way to Beltway 8.

GOLF   Houston proper has public golf courses at most of the city's biggest parks, but with the exception of the Memorial Park Golf Course, the best public courses are outside the city. Probably the best public course (and one of the most difficult) in the area is the **Tournament Players Course at the Woodlands,** located 25 miles north of Houston in The Woodlands (☎ 281/367-1100) and home to Shell Houston Open. Greens fees range from $85 to $95 (cart included); tee times must be made at least 3 days in advance. One of the loveliest and well-respected courses in the area is the **Longwood Golf Club,** 13300 Longwood Trace in Cypress, at the northwest edge of Houston; to get there, take Tex. 290 (☎ 281/373-4100). Fees are $55 to $65 (cart included); tee times should be reserved at least 5 days in advance. Another course that a lot of people talk about is **Tour 18,** which copies 18 of the greatest holes in golf. The course is at 3102 FM 1960 in Humble, about 12 miles north of Houston, off Tex. 59 (☎ 281/540-1818). Greens fees are $60 to $140 (cart included); reserve a tee time at least a week in advance.

In town, there's **Memorial Park Golf Course** (☎ 713/862-4033), one of the top-10 courses in the area. Greens fees are $22.50 to $32, and you can reserve a tee time 3 days in advance. **Hermann Park's golf course** is centrally located (☎ 713/526-0077), with greens fees ranging from $32 to $41. You can reserve a tee time 3 days in advance. At both the Memorial Park and Hermann Park courses, there's an extra $10 to $15 fee for reservations more than 3 days in advance.

TENNIS   Of course, the best strategy to get some tennis in is to stay at a hotel with courts. **Memorial Park** has some of the best of the public courts; make reservations well in advance by calling ☎ 713/867-0440.

SPECTATOR SPORTS

If you're in Houston and decide on the spur of the moment to try to get tickets to a game, you can call **Ticket Stop,** 5925 Kirby Dr. #D (☎ 713/526-8889), a private ticket agency. They charge extra for the tickets, so if possible, it's best to buy direct or in advance.

AUTO RACING   Every year in September, Houston hosts the **Texaco Havoline Grand Prix,** a race through the city's downtown streets that's part of the CART circuit. For information and tickets, call ☎ **713/739-7272** or visit www.texacogp.com.

BASEBALL   **Houston Astros** fans are enjoying the new downtown stadium, **Enron Field,** with its retractable roof that's open mostly in the early part of the season before the weather gets too hot. With a little planning, tickets aren't hard to come by; call ☎ **713/627-8767** or visit www.astros.com.

BASKETBALL   The **Houston Rockets** play at the **Compaq Center** in Greenway Plaza, located off of the Southwest Freeway between downtown and the Loop. This is a popular team, and tickets must be purchased well in advance to get anything approaching good seats (☎ **713/627-3865;** www.nba.com/rockets). The women's team, the **Comets,** has dominated the WNBA and is very popular with local sports fans. The Comets play at the Compaq Center, too. For ticket info, call ☎ **713/627-9622** or look them up online at www.wnba.com/comets.

GOLF TOURNAMENTS   The **Shell Houston Open** happens in The Woodlands in late April. For information and tickets, call ☎ **281/367-7999.**

GREYHOUND RACING   **Gulf Greyhound Park,** located off the Gulf Freeway between Houston and Galveston via Exit 15 (☎ **800/275-2946;** www.gulfgreyhound.com), offers racing year-round six times a week. Admission costs $1.

HOCKEY   The **Houston Aeros,** of the International Hockey League, play at the Compaq Center; tickets are usually not difficult to obtain. Call ☎ **713/627-2376** or visit www.aeros.com.

HORSE RACING   **Sam Houston Race Park,** 7575 N. Sam Houston Parkway (☎ **800/807-7223** or 281/807-7223; www.shrp.com), is in northwest Houston on Beltway 8 between where it crosses Tex. 290 and I-45. Quarter horse racing is from June to September; thoroughbred racing is from October to March. General admission is $3 for adults, $1 for seniors. Races are most weekends (Thursday through Sunday).

MARATHONS   The **Houston Methodist Marathon** occurs in January and attracts more than 6,000 entrants from around the world. Call ☎ **713/957-3453** for more information.

RODEO   Houstonians go all out "Western" for a couple of weeks every February when the **Houston Livestock Show and Rodeo** takes place. Billed as the largest event of its kind, the Rodeo fills the **Astrodome** (it will be moved to the new football stadium in 2003), where aside from the usual events like bull riding and calf roping, there are performances by famous country-and-western artists. Call ☎ **713/791-9000** for more information.

5 Shopping

If you're anywhere in Houston, you probably aren't far from a mall, of which there are many more than can be mentioned here. They're usually located at or near an intersection of a freeway with the Loop or Beltway 8 or other major artery. These are good for general shopping, but hold little of interest for most visitors. A different story is the outlet malls, the principal one being **Katy Mills** out at the far western boundary of Houston, in the town of Katy. Take the Katy Freeway (I-10 west) until you spot the signs. This mall is a mammoth collection of about 200 factory outlet stores that offer a large selection of merchandise at discount prices. The size of the discount varies; some are good deals. There are also restaurants and a large movie theater present.

Whether you're a purposeful shopper or a last-minute accidental one, you'll need to know something about the shopping terrain of Houston. Of course, the main shopping area in Houston is Uptown, but other areas have a diversity of offerings that might prove to be just what you're looking for.

DOWNTOWN

The oldest of Houston's department stores, **Foley's,** still has its original store on Main Street at Lamar (☎ 713/405-7035). It's a large five-story building that occupies an entire block. It carries several lines of expensive clothing and perfumes as well as some moderately priced ones. The other happy shopping ground downtown is **The Park Shops,** 1200 McKinney, across the street from the Four Seasons Hotel (☎ 713/759-1442). It's a group of about 40 small stores, mostly boutiques and specialty shops.

EAST END

Just the other side of the freeway from the George Brown Convention Center is a commercial **Chinatown,** where you can find all kinds of goods imported from across Asia. Furniture, foods, curios—you can browse your way through a number of little import stores, all within a 4-block area, between Dowling on the east, Chartreuse on the west, Rusk on the north, and Dallas on the south.

MONTROSE

Along Westheimer from Woodhead to Mandell you'll find several antiques and junk shops that are perfect for the leisurely shopper who's out to find a diamond in the rough. If after browsing through these you haven't had your fill, there is a grouping of similar stores on 19th Street in the Heights. (For the more discriminating antiques stores go to the Kirby District.) Don't ever accept the first price you're offered at these places—they almost always will lower the price. Also along Westheimer are a number of vintage clothing stores that offer some entertaining shopping. North of Westheimer, on West Gray where it intersects with Shepherd, a whole different sort of shopping awaits at the **River Oaks Shopping Center.** This is Houston's oldest shopping center. It's two blocks long and extends down both sides of West Gray in white-and-black art deco. It's a tony collection of galleries, boutiques, antiques shops, and specialty stores as well as some fine restaurants and an art cinema.

KIRBY DISTRICT

Kirby is more uniformly upscale than Montrose. Where it begins by Westheimer there are a couple of strip malls, the largest of which is **Highland Village,** 4000 Westheimer (☎ 713/850-3100). Highland Village, like so much of the retail business in this part of town, is aimed at the upper-middle class shopper with such stores as Williams-Sonoma and Pottery Barn and a few one-of-a-kind boutiques. From this part of Kirby Drive to where it passes the Rice Village, is a section known informally as **Gallery Row.** The Row has a mix of galleries, designer showrooms, and shops of antiques and special furnishings. And finally, there's **the Village,** a 16-block neighborhood of small shops now mixed with outlets from high-dollar national retailers. A few of the small shops are survivors from simpler times that are now a bit at odds with their new environment of day spas, expensive shoe stores, and famous designer boutiques. There are also various restaurants to choose from in the Village when it's time to take a break from browsing.

UPTOWN

To start with there's **the Galleria,** 5075 Westheimer (☎ **713/622-0663**), which occupies a long stretch of land along Westheimer and Post Oak. It has 320 stores including big department stores such as Saks Fifth Avenue, Lord & Taylor, and Neiman Marcus, and small designer retailers such as Gucci, Emporio Armani, and Dolce & Gabbana. Across Westheimer from the Galleria is another shopping center called **Centre at Post Oak,** with stores such as FAO Schwarz and Barnes & Noble Booksellers. If you're in Uptown and are looking for the finest in Western wear, go to **Stelzig of Texas,** 3123 Post Oak (☎ **281/629-7779**). This store has been selling clothing, saddles, and other Western goods to Houstonians for generations.

7

Houston After Dark

*W*hether you're looking for world-class opera or a night of dancing, this chapter will help you take advantage of Houston's many entertainment options.

1 The Performing Arts

For fans of the performing arts, Houston is fertile ground. Few cities in the country can equal it in the quality of its resident orchestra, opera, ballet, and theater companies. In addition, there are several organizations that bring talented artists and companies here from around the country and the world, presenting everything from Broadway shows to Argentine tango groups to string quartets. Tickets aren't usually discounted for the opera, ballet, or symphony, but you should ask anyway. For information about performances, visit the websites of the various organizations listed below. For quick, though incomplete, listings of performances, go to the visitor's center website, **www.houston-guide.com**.

The symphony, the ballet, the opera, and the Alley Theatre (the city's largest and oldest theater company), all hold their performances in the theater district downtown. The opera and the ballet share the Wortham Center (and have the same ticket phone line); the symphony plays at Jones Hall, a block away; and the Alley Theatre is one of those rare companies that actually owns its own theater, located cater-corner from the symphony. Also in the theater district is the Aerial Theater, which hosts a wide variety of musical and dramatic acts and the soon to be completed Hobby Performing Arts Center, which will be shared by the Society for Performing Arts and Theater Under the Stars.

The Society for the Performing Arts (SPA), 615 Louisiana St. (box office ☎ **713/227-4772**), is a large nonprofit organization that brings to Houston distinguished dance companies, jazz bands, theater productions, and soloists.

Within SPA, there's a program called the Broadway Series, which brings popular productions from Broadway and London's West End to Houston. The organization uses Jones Hall and the Wortham Center (and soon the Hobby Performing Arts Center). For information, visit www. spahouston.org. Tickets for the Broadway Series must be purchased through **Ticketmaster** at (☎ 713/629-3700) or online at www.ticketmaster.com. You can purchase tickets to other SPA events from Ticketmaster, but you'll save money by buying them directly from the SPA.

Following are brief descriptions of the principal organizations; there are many more, especially independent theater companies that present several plays a year.

CLASSICAL MUSIC, OPERA & BALLET

The **Houston Symphony** (☎ 713/224-7575; www. houstonsymphony.org) is the city's oldest performing arts organization. Its season is from September to May, during which it holds about 100 concerts in Jones Hall at 615 Louisiana. The classical series usually contains a number of newer compositions with visits by several guest conductors and soloists from around the world. There is also a pops series and a chamber music series, which often holds its performances at Rice University.

Da Camara of Houston (☎ 713/524-5050; www. dacamara.com) brings classical and jazz chamber music orchestras to the city and holds concerts either at the Wortham or in the lobby of the Menil Collection. You can buy tickets from the box office at 1427 Branard Street in the Montrose area.

The nationally acclaimed **Houston Grand Opera** is the fifth-largest opera company in the United States. Known for being innovative and premiering new operas such as *Nixon in China,* its productions of classical works are brilliant visual affairs. The opera season is from October to May. For tickets and information, visit **www.houston.org** or call ☎ 713/ 227-ARTS at the Wortham Center, 500 Texas Ave.

The **Houston Ballet** (☎ 713/227-ARTS; www. houstonballet.org) has garnered enormous critical acclaim from across the country. A lot of the credit belongs to director Ben Stevenson, who came to Houston more than 25 years ago under the condition that the company create its own school to teach dance as Stevenson believed it should be taught. This school, the **Houston Ballet Academy,** now supplies the company with 90% of its dancers, and its graduates dance in many other top ballet companies. The company tours a great deal but manages around 80 performances a year in Houston.

THEATER

The **Alley Theatre,** 615 Texas Ave. (☎ 713/228-8421; www.alleytheatre.org), has won many awards for its productions. Its home holds a large theater and an arena theater, and during the year the company uses both to stage about 12 different productions, ranging from Shakespeare to Stoppard and even a musical or two. Ask about half-price tickets for sale the day of the show for weekday and Sunday performances.

Theater Under the Stars, 2600 Southwest Fwy. (☎ 800/678-5440; www.tuts.com), specializes in musicals that it either brings to town or produces itself, averaging 200 performances annually. The organization got its name from having first worked at Miller Outdoor Theater in Hermann Park. Now it uses the Wortham Center and will eventually use the new Hobby Center.

The **Ensemble Theater,** 3335 Main St. (☎ 713/520-0055), is the city's largest black theater company. Founded in 1976, the Ensemble has grown from a band of strolling players into a resident professional company of 40 actors and eight directors. Their specialty is African American and experimental theater.

2 The Club & Music Scene

Having a night on the town in Houston doesn't require a lot of planning, but pick up a copy of the *Houston Press,* the free weekly publication that you can find at many restaurants and shops. It provides a good rundown of what musical and comedy acts are in town, and it includes a lot of advertising from the clubs. There's also the daily newspaper, the *Chronicle,* which has a well-organized entertainment section, and a pullout published on Thursdays. If you want to know what's going on in the clubs before you get to Houston, try their websites, **www.houstonpress.com** and **www.houstonchronicle.com**.

In general, the most popular locations for nightspots are the following: downtown, around the theater district and Old Market Square; in the Montrose Area; and south of the Galleria along Richmond Avenue (called the Richmond Strip). There are enough clubs in these places that you can move from one to another quickly and easily, and there's enough variety that you can usually find something you like.

MEGACLUBS

Bayou Place. 500 Texas Ave. ☎ **713/230-1666.**

Formerly Houston's convention center, this entertainment complex in the heart of the theater district rents space to several venues. It now houses the **Aerial Theater,** which usually has live music or comedy (call the number above); the **Hard Rock Cafe** (☎ 281/479-7025), with some live acts on the weekends; **Harlon's Bayou Blues** (☎ 713/230-0111), with live blues Thursday through Saturday; and **Slick Willie's** (☎ 713/230-1277), a billiards club. Also, there are a few video and dance bars with canned music that are very popular with a younger crowd. Bayou Place is also home to the **Angelika Film Center and Café** (☎ 713/225-5232), a popular place to hang out in the evening before going clubbing or to a concert.

City Streets. 5078 Richmond Ave. ☎ **713/840-8555.** Cover $3–$5.

This huge complex has six clubs under the same roof: the Rose, a large country-and-western dance hall with recorded music and a full-size replica of the Alamo; the Blue Monkey, a karaoke bar; Stray Cats, where dueling pianists play sing-alongs, perform skits, exchange barbs with each other, and get members of the audience involved, too; Atlantis, a dance club with '70s and '80s music; Cages, an up-to-date music dance club, and Midway, a large billiards club with televised sporting events. City Streets is located at the beginning of the Richmond Strip, near the Loop.

ROCK

Engine Room. 1515 Pease. ☎ **713/654-7846.** Cover $3–$8.

A club that schedules many touring alternative-rock acts, the Engine Room attracts a young, 20-something clientele. It's located at the southeastern edge of downtown, far from most of the other clubs.

Fitzgerald's. 2706 White Oak. ☎ **713/862-3838.** Cover $3–$15.

Centrally located near the Heights in the old Polish Hall, this club features talented local bands and a lot of touring acts. There's also a large dance floor.

JAZZ

Red Cat Jazz Café. 924 Congress. ☎ **713/227-2200.**

The Red Cat is much the same concept as Sambucca, but it's less expensive and attracts a younger, less-formal crowd. On weekends there's a $10 minimum.

Sambucca Jazz Café. 909 Texas Ave. ☎ **713/224-5299.**

This expensive jazz supper club lines up great performers nightly for a dressy and prosperous clientele.

Scott Gertner's Skybar. 3400 Montrose Blvd. ☎ **713/520-9688.** Cover $7–$10.

This venue atop a 10-story building at the corner of Montrose and Hawthorne is a lovely place to hear jazz. Scott Gertner and his six-piece band play upbeat contemporary swing on Wednesdays, Fridays, and Saturdays; on other nights the bands vary. The club has a dance floor and a terrace.

BLUES

Big Easy Social and Pleasure Club. 5731 Kirby Dr. ☎ **713/523-9999.** Cover $5–$15.

This club lines up a lot of local blues talent that is uncommonly good, as well as touring acts. The clientele is a real mix of everything from yuppies to bikers.

Billy Blues. 6025 Richmond Dr. ☎ **713/266-9294.** Cover $10–$15 Wed–Sat.

One of the many clubs along the Richmond Strip, this one sets itself apart by signing up very good blues acts from around the country. Monday and Tuesday are open-mic nights with some good local talent and no cover charge.

FOLK & ACOUSTIC

Anderson Fair. 2007 Grant. ☎ **713/528-8576.** Cover $7–$10.

This folk and acoustic club is a survivor from the '60s, and looks every bit the product of its age. In its many years, it has nurtured several folk artists who went on to become big names in folk, including Nancy Griffith. That it opens only Fridays and Saturdays only adds to its aura of counterculture. It's located 1 block off Montrose, behind the Montrose Art Supply building.

✪   McGonigels Mucky Duck. 2425 Norfolk. ☎ **713/528-5999.** Cover under $10.

A folk and bluegrass institution in Houston, the Mucky Duck offers pub grub and burgers, wine and beer, and live music every night (except Sunday, when it's closed). Wednesday Irish jam sessions are free, as are Mondays. The club is near Kirby Drive where it intersects the Southwest Freeway.

COUNTRY & WESTERN
✪   Blanco's. 3406 West Alabama. ☎ **713/439-0072.** Cover $8–$15 Thurs–Fri. Closed on Saturdays for private parties.

This Texas-style honky-tonk packs 'em in Monday through Friday, attracting all sorts, from River Oaks types to tool pushers. Lots of good Texas bands like to play here, so it's a great opportunity to see a well-known band in a small venue. There's a midsize dance floor. Monday to Wednesday is open-mic night, usually with one or another local band.

The Firehouse Saloon and Eatery. 5930 Southwest Fwy. ☎ **713/ 977-1962.** Cover $5–$10 Thurs–Sat.

Live music from Tuesday to Saturday brings customers out to dance the two-step. Local and touring bands from across the southwest provide the music.

DANCE CLUBS
Poly Esther's Culture Club. 6111 Richmond Ave. ☎ **713/279-1977.** Cover $6.

Go back to the '70s and '80s if you dare. This club, popular with singles and a wide range of ages, is full of icons from that era, and you can expect to dance to a lot of disco and pop music along the lines of early Madonna.

Spy. 112 Travis St. ☎ **713/225-2229.** Cover $10.

One of the first clubs to set up downtown, it's still very popular with the 20- and 30-something crowd, and there are a lot of singles. Music varies, depending on the night and the DJ, but it's mostly Euro, techno, and a little hip-hop.

A COMEDY CLUB
Laff Stop. 1952-A West Gray. ☎ **713/524-2333.** Cover $10–$20.

By far the best place for stand-up in Houston, though many of the acts have a biting edge and are not appropriate for kids; call before you go. There are usually three to four acts a night.

3 The Bar Scene

TAVERNS

La Carafe. 813 Congress. ☎ **713/229-9399.**

La Carafe has been around for ages, and the small, two-story brick building it occupies, even longer. In fact, it is the oldest commercial building in the city and sits slightly askew on a tiny lot facing Old Market Square. The jukebox is something of a relic, too, with the most eclectic mix possible and some obscure choices. The clientele is mostly older downtowners who were here before the resurgence, mostly office types, in-line skaters, and reporters from the *Chronicle.* For sheer character, no place can beat it.

Marfreless. 2006 Peden (in the River Oaks Shopping Center). ☎ **713/528-0083.**

This is the perfect dark bar for intimate conversation over drinks. The background music is always classical, and the ambiance is understated. Little alcoves here and there are considered romantic. The only trouble is finding the bar. If you stand facing the River Oaks Theater, walk left then make a right into the parking lot. Look for an unmarked door under a metal stairway.

SPORTS BARS

Dave and Buster's. 6010 Richmond Ave. ☎ **713/952-2233.**

This is the large version of a sports bar, with several screens and lots of pool tables. It can handle a large crowd that enjoys a game of pool with a background of several sporting events—unless there's a particularly big game on, when the crowd becomes focused and drops their pool cues.

Grif's. 3416 Roseland. ☎ **713/528-9912.** Located in the Montrose area; take Montrose to Hawthorne (2 blocks south of Westheimer), turn east, then make a right on Roseland.

This is the archetypal sports bar before they became super large, high-tech, multiscreen palaces. It has been in business since the '60s and it has the worn-in look to show for it. The friendly crowd includes many regulars. TV, dartboards, beer by the pitcher—it's an honest example of the American equivalent of the quintessential British pub. Be prepared to talk sports.

4 Gay & Lesbian Nightlife

The Montrose area is where most of Houston's gay nightlife is centered. There are more than a dozen gay bars and clubs mostly along lower Westheimer Road and Pacific Street. For current news, pick up a copy of *Houston Voice.*

Club Rainbow. 1417-B Westheimer. ☎ **713/522-5166.**

This is a friendly lesbian bar frequented by couples and singles from all walks of life. It has a popular dance floor and plays a variety of music.

EJ's. 2517 Ralph. ☎ **713/527-9071.**

In the Montrose area, just north of the 2500 block of Westheimer, there is a low-key but popular bar. Gay men of all ages come for drinks and, perhaps, a game of pool. There's also a dance floor, and a small stage for the occasional drag show.

Rich's. 2401 San Jacinto. ☎ **713/759-9606.** Cover $10.

A large and popular dance club in the midtown area south of downtown, Rich's gets a mixed crowd that's mostly gay men and women. It's noted for its lights and decorations and a large dance floor with a mezzanine level. It's very popular on Saturdays.

Side Trips in East Texas

*E*ast Texas—which borders Louisiana from the coastal cities of Beaumont, Port Arthur, and Houston all the way north to where the state meets Arkansas—has lovely national forests and state parks and several rivers and lakes, and it's visited more by campers and fishermen than any other species of traveler. East Texas towns are not the region's main draw, and most Texans find humor in the idea of tourism in places like Beaumont or Port Arthur. Nice places to live, perhaps, but not places to go out of one's way to visit.

1 Beaumont & Port Arthur

If you drive east on I-10 from Houston towards New Orleans, you'll arrive in **Beaumont** in 1½ hours. Beaumont is a coastal city and inland port, a refinery town and manufacturing center, with a population of 120,000. If you continue along the interstate, after 20 minutes you'll reach the refinery town of **Orange** (pop. 20,000) on the Louisiana border. If, instead of continuing east from Beaumont you exit onto Tex. 96 and go southeast toward the coast, in 20 minutes you'll arrive in **Port Arthur** (pop. 60,000), another refinery town and port on Lake Sabine. This area isn't the prettiest part of east Texas, but it is the most urban and economically active. This fact led boosters of these three cities to dub the area the "Golden Triangle," for which they caught plenty of abuse from other Texans because of the gaping chasm between reality and propaganda. As you may find when you visit these cities, *golden* is the last adjective to come to mind. They have since toned it down to the "Cajun Triangle," underlining the fact that much of the population is Cajun, having moved here from southwest Louisiana during the oil boom early in the century.

It was just outside of Beaumont, on a rise of land called Spindletop, where drillers struck the world's first true gusher in 1901, thereby initiating the long association of Texas with oil. A large granite monument to the well lies south of town just off the highway to Port Arthur. Other attractions include a small fire-fighting museum and a museum dedicated to Babe Didrikson Zaharias, a native of Beaumont and considered by many to be the most amazing woman athlete of the century. (She dominated the women's golf tour, was all American in basketball, and held world records in several track and field events.) For information on these and other area attractions, contact the **Beaumont Convention & Visitors Bureau,** 801 Main St., Beaumont (☎ **409/880-3749** or 800/392-4401), open weekdays from 8am to 5pm. If time is not on your side, you will probably want to drive right on through Beaumont, but should you need a place to spend the night, the national chains are represented mostly along I-10, including a **Hilton,** 2355 I-10 (☎ **800/HILTONS**), and an upscale **Holiday Inn,** 3950 I-10 (☎ **800/HOLIDAY**).

Port Arthur is much like Beaumont, only smaller, and like Beaumont, it has a famous daughter—the '60s blues singer and icon Janis Joplin. She doesn't have her own museum, but the **Museum of the Gulf Coast,** 700 Proctor St. (☎ **409/982-7000**), has an exhibit honoring her, including a replica of her psychedelic Porsche, her album covers, and several personal possessions. The museum also displays exhibits on the geography and early history of the area, as well as a collection of artwork by Port Arthur native Robert Rauschenberg, the painter. The museum is open Monday to Saturday 9am to 5pm, Sunday 1pm to 5pm; admission is $3.50 for adults, $1.50 for children.

2 Piney Woods & Big Thicket National Preserve

If from Beaumont you drive north on Tex. 96 (or from Houston you drive north on I-45 or Tex. 59), you would soon enter the forestland known in Texas as the **Piney Woods.** This is a lovely part of the state that stretches all the way north to Arkansas. In the thickest part of the Piney Woods are four national forests and the Big Thicket National Preserve. In and around these forests are ponds, lakes, and reservoirs that enhance the beauty of the region and provide opportunities for boating, canoeing, swimming, and fishing. Another attractive quality of these lands is that they are relatively less visited than national parks and forests in other states, yet they are very close to Houston and Beaumont.

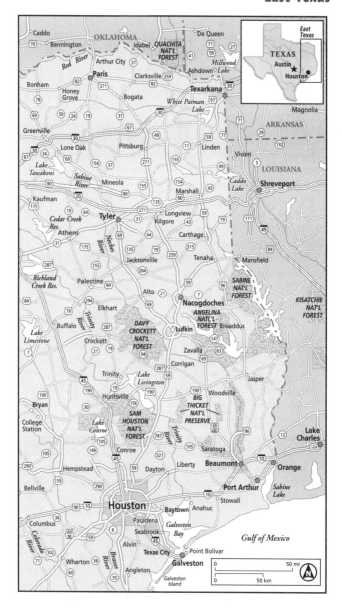

The **Big Thicket** is a watery lowland forest jammed with dense underbrush and permeated by swamps, sloughs, and creeks. The early settlers, for whom it was inhospitable and impassable, did not appreciate it. Occasionally, it provided a hiding place for outlaws. With lumbering, oil exploration, roads, and settlement, the Big Thicket has been reduced to a tenth of its original size. Of what's left, 100,000 acres have been preserved by acts of Congress.

The federal government stepped in to preserve the area because the Big Thicket represents a complex habitat of varying ecological niches rich in diverse species of plant life. This complexity is rare and unlike what you'll see in the rest of the Piney Woods, which is predominantly pine-forest habitat that, as you move west, gradually gives way to oak. In the Big Thicket you'll find magnolia, cypress, hickory trees, and many species of flowering plants, including several insect eaters. The preserved area is not one large expanse of land but 15 separate units. Most of the preserved land follows waterways such as the Neches River. One of the largest parcels is directly north of Beaumont, as is the **information station** for the preserve (7 miles north of the town of Kountze on FM 420). The station is open daily and has maps and info on hiking and boating. It also offers ranger-guided tours of the area that can be quite informative; contact the office in Beaumont at ☎ **409/246-2337** or www.nps.gov/bith. Several canoe rental services are available in season. If you'd like to camp, there are limited primitive camping sites available; inquire at the information station.

3 Alabama & Coushatta Indian Reservation

Two hours north of Houston, adjacent to one of the large Big Thicket preserves, lies the **Alabama & Coushatta Indian Reservation.** The Alabama and Coushatta were forest-dwelling tribes of the eastern United States who were pushed westward by the expansion of the white settlers. When Texas won its independence from Mexico, they were given a place to stay by Pres. Sam Houston. Unfortunately, they were never given title and, for a century, had to fight to keep loggers and oil drillers off the land and defeat the government's efforts to move them to Oklahoma. This is one of the few surviving forest reservations. Most of the 900 inhabitants make a living

Texas State Railroad State Historical Park

Thirty miles north of Davy Crockett National Forest, in the town of Rusk, the Parks and Wildlife Department bought a **railroad line** that stretches 25 miles west to the town of Palestine. Steam locomotives pulling vintage railway cars run on these tracks. The train runs on a limited schedule from March through October; the round-trip ride through pine forest costs $20 (free for children under 6) and takes about 4 hours. For general information, call ☎ **903/683-5126;** for reservations, call ☎ **903/683-2561.**

by working outside the reservation. Tourism, however, plays a sizable part of the tribes' income. The price of admission to the reservation includes a bus tour of the Big Thicket, a guided tour of the village, and a narrow-gauge train ride. On the reservation, there's a restaurant, craft store, and campgrounds. The reservation is closed to visitors during the winter. For information and prices, call ☎ **800/444-3507** or 409/ 563-4391, or visit www.alabama-coushatta.com. From Houston, take Tex. 59 north to Livingston. You'll see signs pointing the way to the reservation. In Livingston, take I-190 east 17 miles to the reservation.

4 National Forests

Four national forests occupy 630,000 acres distributed among 12 counties. They are roughly the same size, and all have recreation areas and facilities such as boat ramps, camping grounds, and hiking trails. Little more than an hour away from Houston is **Sam Houston National Forest** (ranger offices are in the town of New Waverly on I-45; ☎ **409/ 344-6205**). Less than an hour north of it is **Davy Crockett National Forest** (ranger offices in Crockett; ☎ **409/ 544-2046**). To the east lies **Angelina National Forest** (ranger office in Lufkin; ☎ **409/639-8620**), and still further east is **Sabine National Forest** (ranger office in Hemphill; ☎ **409/ 787-2791**). Fishing draws most of the people to this area; boats and guides are easy to come by, but you'll need to get a temporary license, which costs $20. If the weather is good, hiking in the Piney Woods can be most pleasant. There's one 126-mile-long hiking trail that crosses Sam Houston National Forest.

5 Caddo Lake & Jefferson

Caddo Lake, picturesque in a primeval way, lies on the state line between Texas and Louisiana. Ancient-looking cypress trees draped in Spanish moss grow along the lake's broken shore, their roots rising from the water in deformed shapes. It's also a lake of narrow channels and small islands offering constantly changing views. A state park on the southern shore of the lake offers cabins, fishing and swimming, boating, and hiking. During the season, visitors can take a steamboat ride offered by the **Caddo Lake Steamboat Company** (☎ **903/ 789-3978**). The trip costs $15 for all ages and lasts 1½ hours. Near the lake is the picturesque town of **Jefferson** (pop. 2,600), which in the mid–19th century, was a boomtown. Half the houses seem to have historical plaques, and many of these are B&Bs or small hotels. (In fact, the lodging business seems to be the major economic force here with almost 60 B&Bs.) For a list of these, as well as information on tours (historical tour of Jefferson, historic homes tour, and a riverboat tour of Big Cypress Bayou), contact the **Marion County Chamber of Commerce** at ☎ **888/GO-RELAX** or 903/665-2672, or visit **www.jefferson-texas.com**.

9

Galveston

*G*alveston, a prosperous port throughout most of the 19th century, is located 50 miles from Houston on a barrier island directly across from the mainland coast of Texas. One of its main attractions is the downtown historic district with its Victorian commercial buildings and houses. Another is the beaches, which draw Houstonians and other Texans in droves during the summer. Galveston is a good destination for families, or, for anyone who is overwhelmed by Houston; it's a quiet town with many points of interest including Moody Gardens and the tall ship *Elissa,* and it's not far from NASA and Kemah.

1 Essentials

GETTING THERE

The best way to reach Galveston is by car. To get to Galveston from downtown Houston, take the Gulf Freeway (I-45 south). After crossing over to Galveston, the interstate becomes Broadway, Galveston's principal street.

ORIENTATION

Broadway, Galveston's main street, doesn't cut directly across the island to the seashore; instead it slants eastward and arrives at the seashore on the east end of the island, in front of Stewart Beach. Streets crossing Broadway are numbered; those parallel to Broadway have letters or names.

The East End Historic District and the old Strand District are north of Broadway. The Historic District is the old silk-stocking neighborhood that runs from 9th to 19th Streets between Broadway and Church Street. It has many lovely houses that have been completely restored. Three large mansions-turned-museums have regular tours (see "Exploring Galveston," below), and the city's historical preservation society holds tours of several private houses in May (inquire at the visitor center). The Strand District is the restored commercial district that runs between 19th and 25th Streets between Church Street and the harbor piers. When cotton was king, Galveston was a booming port and commercial center, and the Strand was dubbed the "Wall Street of the Southwest." What you see now are three- and four-story buildings along 6 blocks of the Strand and along some of the side streets; many of these are Victorian iron-fronts, called this because the facades included structural and decorative ironwork. This was a common building practice before the turn of the century, but you won't find a better-preserved collection of these types of buildings anywhere else in the United States. Nowadays, the Strand is a shopping and dining area that offers a wide variety of stores.

VISITOR INFORMATION

If you're planning a trip, check the Galveston Convention & Visitors Bureau's website at **www.galvestoncvb.com** or call ☎ **888/GAL-ISLE.** If you're in town already, visit their information center at 2428 Seawall Blvd., close to 25th Street (☎ **409/763-4311**). It's open Monday through Saturday 9am to 5pm.

GETTING AROUND

Most of Galveston's hotels, motels, and restaurants are located along the seawall from where Broadway meets the shore all the way west past 60th Street. As of summer 2001, a **shuttle bus** provides transportation between this hotel strip and the other two most visited areas, the Strand and Moody Gardens. The fare is $1; contact the visitors center for more information. If you're on the seawall around 25th Street (near the visitors center), you can take the **Galveston Island Rail Trolley** to the Strand District. The fare is 60¢ from the seawall to the Strand, but for a ride just around the Strand, it's free.

2 Exploring Galveston

The beaches are always Galveston's most popular attraction. They may not measure up to those of the most popular beach destinations, the sand is a light tan color instead of white, but it's all sand and no rocks, and while the water isn't turquoise, it's at a wonderful temperature for much of the year. **East**

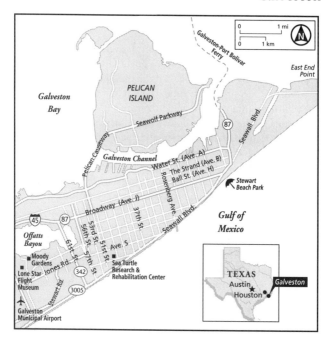

Beach and **Stewart Beach,** operated by the city, have pavilions with dressing rooms, showers, and restrooms, ideal for day-trippers. Stewart Beach is located at the end of Broadway, and East Beach is about a mile east of Stewart Beach. There's a $5 per vehicle entrance fee. Most other beaches are free; many of the nicest are on the west side of the island. Another activity, popular with visitors and locals alike, is to walk, skate, or ride a bike atop the seawall, which extends 10 miles along the coast.

Unlike Houston, there are many tours offered here: **Galveston Harbour Tours** (☎ **409/765-1700**) offers a Saturday morning dolphin watch tour and a more frequent harbor tour; **Duck Tours** (☎ **409/621-4771**) offers bus tours of the island; and **Ghost Tours** (☎ **409/949-2027**) offers a walking tour of the Strand District. On Broadway, there are a few massive 19th-century mansions that offer tours: **Ashton Villa,** 2328 Broadway (☎ **409/762-3933**);

The Storm

At the end of the nineteenth century, Galveston was a thriving port and a fast-growing city with a bright future. In fact, it was the largest city in Texas and had the third busiest port in the country. Of course, being on the Gulf meant the possibility of a hurricane, but the prevailing thought was that the shallow bottom on the Texas side of the Gulf of Mexico would prevent the formation of large waves and blunt the force of any approaching storm. Despite the fact that a storm completely wiped out the Texas port town of Indianola in 1886, there was an assumption that Galveston would be safe. More evidence to the contrary came in the form of a massive storm that hit Galveston in September 1900.

The storm came ashore at night with a 20-foot surge that washed completely over the island. Houses were smashed into matchwood, and their dwellers spilled out into the dark waters. By morning, more than 6,000 islanders—one out of every six—were drowned; it was the worst natural disaster ever to

the **Bishop's Palace,** 1402 Broadway (☎ **409/762-2475**); and the **Moody Mansion,** 2618 Broadway (☎ **409/ 762-7668**). Call for rates and additional information.

MUSEUMS

Except for Moody Gardens and its neighbor, the **Lone Star Flight Museum** (see review below), all of Galveston's museums are in and around the Strand, the old commercial center. Highlights include **Pier 21 Theater** (☎ **409/763-8808**), which shows a short documentary about the 1900 storm that devastated the town, and another about a one-time Galveston resident, the pirate Jean Laffite. On the same pier are the **Texas Seaport Museum** (☎ **409/763-1877**) and the *Elissa,* a restored tall ship. Admission is $6 for adults, $4 for children under 13. Next door, at Pier 19, is a one-of-a-kind museum about offshore drilling rigs. You will probably have noticed that around the harborside area next to the Strand, the most eye-catching objects in view are the massive offshore rigs that are often parked on the other side of Galveston's ship channel. Mostly, these mammoth constructions come to the Port of strike the United States. The city's population dropped even further when many of those that survived were left destitute and preferred to rebuild their lives on safer shores. Those who remained went to work to prevent a reoccurrence of the disaster. Galveston erected a stout seawall that now stretches 10 miles along the shore with several jetties made of large blocks of granite projecting out into the sea. It also filled in land under the entire city, raising it 17 feet in some places and jacking up all the surviving houses to the new level. But, despite all the effort, Galveston would never regain its momentum. The memory of "the storm" proved too compelling for many of the region's merchants to reestablish themselves in Galveston. Instead, they sought the safety of an inland port and provided much impetus for the dredging of the Houston Ship Channel, which was completed in 1914. And in this way, "the storm" rewrote the destinies of these two Texas cities.

Galveston to be reconditioned. Since they spend most of their time far offshore, one doesn't see them often, but here in Galveston you have an opportunity to view one, the **Ocean Star** (☎ **409/766-STAR**), a rig converted into a museum. Through a short film, scale models, actual drilling equipment, and interactive displays, every aspect of the drilling process is explored, including the many rather daunting engineering challenges. Those with a grasp of technical and engineering issues will enjoy this museum the most, but others will appreciate the broader aspects and the sheer size of these constructions. Hours for this and the other museums around the Strand are roughly the same, from 10am to 4pm daily (5pm in summer).

Moody Gardens. 1 Hope Blvd. ☎ **800/582-4673.** www. moodygardens. com. Admission to aquarium $11 adults and students over 13, $9.25 seniors, $6.25 children ages 4–12, free for children 3 and under; admission to each of the following: rain forest pyramid, discovery pyramid, IMAX 3D, and IMAX RIDEFILM $7.50 adults and students, $6.25 seniors, $5.25 children ages 4–12, free for children 3 and under; day passes sometimes available. Daily 10am–9pm in summer; Sun–Thurs 10am–6pm and Fri–Sat 10am–9pm rest of year.

Moody Gardens, an education/entertainment museum, is easily recognizable for its three large glass pyramids. The first one built was the rain forest pyramid, which holds trees, plants, birds, fish, and butterflies from several different rain-forest habitats. A stroll through the building will fascinate anyone who has never been in a rain-forest environment, and the unusual species of Amazonian fish, birds, and butterflies are not often seen in zoos. The aquarium pyramid displays life from four of the world's oceans: penguins from Antarctica, harbor seals from the northern Pacific, and Caribbean and South Pacific reef dwellers. There's also a petting aquarium for those who feel compelled to touch the little darlings. The discovery pyramid displays space exploration but doesn't come close to the nearby Space Center Houston. Also of note are the two IMAX theaters: one is 3D and the other is a Ridefilm. On top of all this, there is a pool and white-sand beach for children and parents and an old paddlewheel boat that journeys out into the bay. There's also a large hotel and spa on the grounds.

Just down the road at 2002 Terminal Drive is the **Lone Star Flight Museum** (☎ **409/740-7106**). It has two hangars filled with aircraft in various states of reconstruction. Many of the planes are from World War II. Admission is $6 for adults, $4 for children ages 4 to 13, free for children 3 and under.

3   Where to Stay

All the economical hotel/motel chains have properties in Galveston, with higher prices for lodgings along the seawall. Of the big chains, **La Quinta Galveston,** 1402 Seawall Blvd. (☎ **800/531-5900**), ranks high; it was completely remodeled last year. Galveston also has a dozen B&Bs, most of which are in Victorian-era houses. The most unusual of these is actually a boat tied to a pier, **The Stacia Leigh B&B** aboard the *Chryseis* (☎ **409/750-8858**; www.stacia-leigh.com). The owners renovated and modified a large yacht built in 1906 for the European industrialist Louis Renault.

Harbor House. No. 28, Pier 21, Galveston, TX 77550. ☎ **800/874-3721** or 409/763-3321. Fax 409/765-6421. www.harborhousePier21.com. 42 units. A/C TV TEL. $105–$185 double. Packages available. AE, DC, DISC, MC, V. Parking $5.

A very different kind of hotel for Galveston, the Harbor House is built on a pier overlooking the harbor instead of a beach. It's actually an excellent location, near the Strand District and next to a few restaurants and museums that have taken over some of the neighboring piers. The architecture and exterior design are quite different as well. Rooms are large and well appointed in modern style without a lot of clutter. Bleached wood floors, Berber carpets, and exposed wood and steel superstructure are design highlights. Offerings include nine marina slips and free continental breakfast. There is no restaurant, but, with so many restaurants within 2 blocks of the hotel, it isn't missed.

Hotel Galvez. 2024 Seawall Blvd., Galveston, TX 77550. ☎ **800/WYNDHAM** or 409/765-7721. Fax 409/765-5780. www.wyndham.com. 231 units. A/C TV TEL. $115–$245 double. Extra person $20. Packages available. AE, DC, DISC, MC, V. Valet parking $7; self-parking free.

Galveston's historic grand hotel, the Galvez has been thoroughly renovated to make the guest rooms more comfortable and to correct the mistakes of previous renovations. Rooms are spacious, well furnished, and conservatively decorated. Marble bathrooms come with hair dryers; other amenities include coffeemaker, iron and ironing board, robes, and dataports. The hotel also offers a restaurant, bar, room service, an outdoor pool with swim-up bar, golf privileges at a local country club, concierge, and a gift shop.

4 Where to Dine

Seafood is why people come to Galveston, and there's quite a variety. There are local representatives of chain restaurants such as Landry's and Joe's Crab Shack, which do a credible job, but, for the best of Galveston's seafood, try one of the places listed below. If you're craving steak, the best in town is **The Steakhouse** in the San Luis Resort, 5222 Seawall Blvd. (☎ **409/744-1500**).

Gaidos. 3800 Seawall Blvd. ☎ **409/762-9625.** Reservations not accepted. Main courses $14–$33; complete dinners $19–$29. AE, DISC, MC, V. Daily 11:45am–10:30pm. Closes an hour or two earlier during low season.

This restaurant is a Galveston tradition that has been owned and operated by the Gaido family for four generations. The

Gaidos have maintained quality by staying personally involved in all aspects of the restaurant—thus the seafood is fresh and the service attentive. The soups and side dishes are mostly traditional Southern and Gulf Coast recipes that are comfort food for the longtime customers. Main dishes include a few chicken, pork, and beef items but the majority are seafood. The menu varies seasonally. The dining room is large, with tables well spread out. There is a large bar area for people waiting for a table.

Saltwater Grill. 2017 Post Office St. ☎ **409/762-FISH.** Reservations recommended. Main courses $12–$27. AE, CB, DC, MC, V. Mon–Fri 11am–2pm; Mon–Thurs 5–10pm; Fri–Sat 5–11pm; Sun 5–9pm. Free parking in rear.

The seafood is quite fresh, and the preparation shows a light touch. The restaurant prints up a menu daily that usually includes some inventive seafood pasta dishes, perhaps a gulf red snapper pan-sautéed and topped with lump crabmeat, a fish dish with an Asian bent, gumbo and/or bouillabaisse, and a few nonseafood options. On a recent trip, the starters were excellent. Situated in an old building near the Strand, the dining room has a pleasant mix of past and present, formal and informal.

Shrimp 'n' Stuff. 3901 Ave. O. ☎ **409/763-2805.** Reservations not accepted. Main courses $7–$10. AE, DC, MC, V. Sun–Thurs 10:30am–8pm; Fri–Sat 10:30am–9pm.

This small, unassuming restaurant where you order at the counter, is thought by many locals to serve the best seafood for the money. The seafood is mostly fried Southern-style and served with hush puppies. Especially popular are the oyster and the shrimp Po'boys, the fried shrimp and the seafood platter.

10

The Texas Gulf Coast

*W*arm year-round temperatures and the blue-green waters of the Gulf of Mexico make this region the vacationland of Texas. This is where Texans come to escape the crowds and stress of Houston and Dallas and the icy winter cold of Amarillo, and where even the locals believe that every day is a holiday.

The Texas Gulf Coast gives us wonderful beaches like Padre Island National Seashore and South Padre Island, with deep-sea fishing, boating, swimming, and even surfing. In addition, this region is one of the premier bird-watching areas in America, with a number of wildlife refuges and other sites where you might spy species of birds seen nowhere else in the United States. One warning, though: The conditions that bring numerous birds here also attract another smaller but extremely annoying species of wildlife, so those planning trips to the coast need to carry plenty of mosquito repellent.

Corpus Christi, the area's largest city, remains a comfortable and inviting community while offering practically all the big-city amenities; and the fishing boats that head into the Gulf of Mexico from Corpus Christi and other port towns each day bring back some of the best seafood you've ever tasted, prepared in innumerable ways at the area's restaurants. Somewhat surprisingly, Gulf Coast communities, such as Rockport, are evolving as art centers, with fine art galleries and a growing number of resident artists. A growing interest in the region's rich history and natural resources has helped produce some fascinating museums. In short, the Gulf Coast offers an escape from the serious side of Texas—the cities with their traffic jams and business suits—and there is plenty more here than just a beach.

1   Corpus Christi

207 miles SW of Houston

This major deepwater seaport—the sixth largest port in the United States by tonnage shipped—is a fun place to visit and a good base for exploring Padre Island and other attractions. With a population of just under 300,000 people, Corpus Christi is the eighth largest city in Texas, but it doesn't feel like a real city. Possibly because of its waterfront and mild weather, Corpus Christi has an appealing small-town atmosphere. Visitors will want to check out the museums, aquarium, and, our favorite stop here, the USS *Lexington* aircraft carrier, and possibly plan a fishing excursion into the bay or out onto the high seas. Then it's time to head to the nearby beaches.

ESSENTIALS
GETTING THERE

Tex. 35 follows the Gulf Coast—albeit slightly inland—from the Houston and Galveston area to Corpus Christi.

The **Corpus Christi International Airport,** located within the city limits on the south side of Tex. 44, west of Padre Island Drive/Tex. 358 (☎ **361/289-0171**), is served by **American Eagle** (☎ **800/433-7300**); **Atlantic Southeast/ Delta** (☎ **800/282-3424**) **Continental/Continental Express** (☎ **800/523-3273**); and **Southwest Airlines** (☎ **800/ 435-9792**).

VISITOR INFORMATION

Contact the **Corpus Christi Convention and Visitors Bureau,** 1201 N. Shoreline (P.O. Box 2664), Corpus Christi, TX 78403 (☎ **800/678-6232** or 361/561-2000; www. corpuschristi-tx-cvb.org). **Visitors centers** (☎ **800/766-2324**) are located at 1823 N. Chaparral, 1433 I-37, and 14252 S. Padre Island Drive.

Corpus Christi's Average Monthly High/Low Temperatures & Precipitation

	Jan	Feb	Mar	Apr	May	June	July	Aug	Sept	Oct	Nov	Dec
High °F	65	69	76	82	86	90	93	93	90	84	76	68
Low °F	45	48	55	63	69	73	75	75	72	64	56	48
Precip.	1.7	2.0	0.9	1.7	3.3	3.4	2.4	3.3	5.5	3.0	1.6	1.3

The Texas Gulf Coast

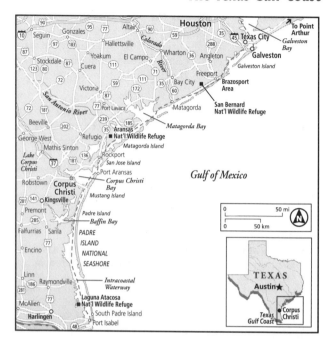

TEXAS

Austin ★

Texas
Gulf Coast   Corpus
Christi

GETTING AROUND

Downtown embraces the intersection of I-37 and Tex. 286, known as the Crosstown Expressway, and continues east to the bay. Shoreline Boulevard runs along the bay, and major downtown arteries leading westward are Main, Leopard, Lipan, Laredo, and Agnes Streets, the latter two being one way in opposite directions. I-37 ends at the Harbor Bridge, which leads to the Texas State Aquarium and USS *Lexington* Floating Museum (see "What to See & Do," below). Major roads leading out of downtown to the south are Staples Street and Port Avenue. The Crosstown Expressway, Tex. 286, intersects south of downtown with South Padre Island Drive, Tex. 358, which crosses the Laguna Madre and leads to Padre Island National Seashore.

FAST FACTS

Health services are available at **Corpus Christi Medical Center** (www.ccmedicalcenter.com), with three locations: Doctors

Regional, 3315 S. Alameda (☎ **361/761-1400**); Bay Area, 7101 S. Padre Island Dr. (☎ **361/761-1200**); and The Heart Hospital, 7002 Williams Dr. (☎ **361/761-1200**). The main **post office,** 802 N. Tancahua St. (1 block north of Leopard Street), is open Monday through Friday from 8am to 5pm.

SPECIAL EVENTS

Bayfest! takes place in early October; the **Texas Jazz Festival** is held during mid- to late October; **Buccaneer Days** are celebrated from late April to early May; the **Bay Jammin' Concerts** are staged Thursday evenings from late May to mid-August; the **C-101 Sand Castle Sculptures** are presented in June; the **Texas Jazz Festival** is held in late July; and the **Harbor Lights Celebration** takes place on the first weekend of December.

WHAT TO SEE & DO

Art Museum of South Texas. 1902 N. Shoreline Blvd. ☎ **361/825-3500.** Fax 361/825-3520. www.stia.org. Admission $3 adults, $2 students, active military personnel, and seniors over 60, free for children 12 and under and for everyone on Thurs. Tues–Sat 10am–5pm, Sun 1–5pm; first Thurs each month 10am–9pm; closed major holidays.

This huge modern art center, operated by the South Texas Institute for the Arts, houses changing exhibits from a variety of mediums, frequently from a historical national and international perspective. There are usually some works from their permanent collection—art of the Americas, mostly Texas and the surrounding states, including northern Mexico—on display, and a small gallery of local artists' works for sale. There is also a gift shop. Lectures, workshops, and musical performances are scheduled regularly; call for the current schedule of events and exhibits.

Asian Cultures Museum & Educational Center. 1809 N. Chaparral St. ☎ **361/882-2641.** www.geocities.com/asiancm. Admission $3 adults, $1 children 12 and under. Tues–Sat 10am–5pm; closed major holidays.

One of only five museums in the United States depicting Asian cultures, this gem is dedicated to increasing public awareness about Asian and Far Eastern cultures. This two-story (there is an elevator) museum contains more than 10,000 square feet of exhibits. You'll see a 5-foot-tall bronze Buddha statue, a Singapore taxicab (bicycle-powered), Kabuki theater dolls, Noh theater masks, and Japanese kimonos, as well as clay circle figures (buried with the remains of the dead). The museum also hosts changing exhibits and special events, such as demonstrations and workshops on Asian crafts and foods, and has a gift shop.

✪ **Corpus Christi Botanical Gardens.** 8545 S. Staples St. ☎ **361/852-2100.** Fax 361/852-7875. Admission $3 adults, $2.50 seniors 65 and over, $1.50 children ages 5–12, free for children under 5. Tues–Sun 9am–5pm; call for holiday hours. Leashed pets allowed.

This series of gardens on a 180-acre site along Oso Creek offers a refreshing escape from the museums and other city attractions of Corpus Christi. Here you can wander among gardens and wetlands and see dozens of tropical hibiscus, exotic bromeliads, cacti, stunning plumeria, and a wide variety of desert and tropical plants. The rose garden contains some 300 roses in a tranquil setting of arbors, trellises, and benches; and there are some 2,000 orchids in a specially constructed orchid greenhouse. The shady Bird & Butterfly Trail meanders through a native south Texas habitat, taking you to an observation tower over Gator Lake, where you'll likely see white pelicans, ducks, egrets, roseate spoonbills, and maybe even the seldom seen, but often talked about, alligator (if he or she really does exist). In addition there is a small gift shop, an art gallery with works by local artists, a playground, and a shaded picnic area.

Corpus Christi Museum of Science & History. 1900 N. Chaparral St. ☎ **361/883-2862.** Admission $8 adults, $7 ages 13–17, $6.50 seniors over 60 and military personnel with ID, $4 ages 5–12, free for children 4 and under. Mon–Sat 10am–5pm, Sun 1–5pm; closed major holidays.

Offering a potpourri of exhibits that detail the land, animals, and humans that make up the Texas Gulf Coast, this well-executed museum runs the gamut from seashells to early American Indians to the numerous plants and animals that call this area home. There's a hands-on hurricane/weather station and an interactive computer station, as well as wildlife dioramas, photos, and more than 1,500 relics from shipwrecks. The Children's Wharf, especially for 3- to 7-year-olds, has a shrimp boat, touch tables, and other exhibits just for kids.

Texas State Aquarium. 2710 N. Shoreline Blvd. ☎ **888/477-4853** or 361/881-1200. www.texasstateaquarium.org. Admission $8.75 adults; $6.75 youths ages 12–17, seniors 60 and older and active military; $5 children ages 4–11; free for children under 4. Additional $3 parking fee. Mon–Sat 9am–5pm, Sun 10–5pm; open until 6pm Memorial Day to Labor Day. Closed Christmas.

This is the place to come to explore the undersea world of the Gulf of Mexico, and you don't even have to get your feet wet!

This state-of-the-art facility offers a wide variety of exhibits, ranging from the Flower Gardens Coral Reef to a sea turtle tank and the swamp exhibit, complete with alligator. You'll see fish and other ocean-dwelling creatures of all varieties—you can pet a shark, if that's what you really want to do—and see close-up a fascinating and colorful world of sea dragons, dwarfs, pipefishes, and more in Seahorse Seatopia. Numerous demonstrations are held throughout the day, such as diving shows and otter and bird feeding. Children enjoy the Octopus Garden Playground, and there's also a gift shop and food court.

✪ USS *Lexington* **Museum on the Bay.** 2914 N. Shoreline Blvd., in Corpus Christi Bay. ☎ **800/523-9539** or 361/888-4873. www.usslexington.com. Admission $9 adults, $4 children ages 4–12, $7 seniors 60 and older and active military with ID, free for children ages 3 and under. Additional $2.50 parking fee. Daily 9am–5pm (last entry 4:30pm).

This floating naval museum was the highlight of our trip to Corpus Christi, in large part because being turned loose in and on a huge World War II–era aircraft carrier is something we had never experienced before, and we found it fascinating. The *Lexington* displaces 42,000 tons and its flight deck measures 910 feet. It had a crew of 1,550 and could travel at over 30 knots. During World War II, the *Lexington* was in almost every major operation in the Pacific Theater, and planes from her decks destroyed 372 enemy aircraft in flight and an additional 475 on the ground. She was dubbed "The Blue Ghost" because of the ship's blue-gray color, and because Japanese propaganda radio broadcaster Tokyo Rose repeatedly and mistakenly announced that the Japanese had sunk the *Lexington*. The *Lexington* was modernized in the 1950s and served in the U.S. Seventh Fleet, including duty during the Vietnam War, and then became a training vessel until being decommissioned in 1991. The USS *Lexington* Museum on the Bay opened in 1992.

Tours of the "Lady Lex," as the carrier is also known, are self-guided, with the aid of a map and strategically placed signs. A video details the history of the ship with historic film footage, and there are a number of exhibits, such as a Navy Seal submarine and interpretive displays of ship engines, plus a flight simulator, that, for $3.50 per person, provides a 5-minute ride simulating the experience of flying, synchronized with a film. However, it is the experience of climbing up and down ladders between decks, seeing the ship's hospital and mess hall, exploring its narrow passages, and imagining what it would be like to live in the claustrophobic conditions of the crew's sleeping quarters that captivated us. On the flight deck are more than a dozen aircraft from the 1930s to the 1960s, including an F-14A Tomcat and a Cobra helicopter. You'll also get a close-up look at the ship's 40-millimeter antiaircraft guns and peer out from the pilothouse and imagine you're at sea. The *Lexington* has a large gift shop and a snack bar.

Note: Although some parts of the USS *Lexington* are easily accessible by anyone, seeing many of the best parts, such as the flight deck, bridge, and engine room involves climbing a lot of steep, old metal stairs and ladders, stepping over metal barricades, and maneuvering through tight passageways. Those with mobility problems will most likely not be able to get to everything.

SPORTS & OUTDOOR PURSUITS

Bird watching, fishing, and water sports are the key outdoor activities in the Corpus Christi area, and some of the best beaches are on nearby Padre Island, which is discussed later in this chapter. Among local parks is the city-maintained **Corpus Christi Beach,** north of Harbor Bridge (☎ **361/884-7275**), with a playground, showers, and picnicking.

BIRD WATCHING   Like most of the Texas Gulf Coast, the Corpus Christi area has great birding opportunities. Among the more than 500 species that have been sighted here are brown pelicans, masked ducks, black-bellied whistling ducks, roseate spoonbills, black-necked stilts, ruby-throated hummingbirds, tri-colored herons, and red-shouldered hawks. Good birding spots include the Corpus Christi Botanical Gardens (see "What to See & Do," above) as well as Blucher Park (downtown at the intersection of Blucher and Carrizo Streets), known for attracting songbirds during their spring and fall migrations. For details on additional bird-watching sites, contact the Corpus Christi Convention and Visitors Bureau (see "Visitor Information," above).

FISHING   This is a wonderful area for both deep-sea and bay fishing. You can cast your line from numerous piers, jetties, and beaches, or head out to sea on a charter or party boat. Charter boats usually cost from $300 to $400 for a full-day trip for one or two people, while party boats are about $60 per person for a full day. There are numerous guides available,

including charter boat services from **Don Hand** (☎ 361/
993-2024), **Salty Aggie Guide Service** (☎ 800/322-3346
or 361/991-6045), **Ingram's Guide Service** (☎ 800/
368-6032 or 361/857-0702), and **Warren Alan's Fishing
Guide Service** (☎ 877/322-7448 or 361/992-2972; www.
texasfishingguides.org/hart). For party boats, try **Copeland's
Marine** (☎ 800/567-5132 or 361/854-1135) or **Captain
Clark Fishing** (☎ 361/884-4369).

WHERE TO STAY
HOTELS, MOTELS, & BED AND BREAKFASTS

Among the numerous national chain motels in Corpus Christi
are **Best Western Garden Inn,** 11217 I-37, exit 11B (☎ 800/
528-1234 or 361/241-6675), with rates for two of $64 to $99;
Best Western Sandy Shores, 3200 Surfside (☎ 800/
528-1234 or 361/883-7456), with rates of $59 to $149 double; **Comfort Suites,** 3925 S. Padre Island Dr. (☎ 800/
228-5150 or 361/225-2500), with rates of $79 to $129 double; **Days Inn,** 4302 Surfside Blvd. (☎ 800/329-7466 or 361/
882-3297), with rates of $40 to $100 double; **Embassy Suites
Hotel,** 4337 S. Padre Island Dr. (☎ 800/362-2779 or 361/
853-7899), with rates for two of $109 to $139; **Holiday Inn
Emerald Beach,** 1102 S. Shoreline Blvd. (☎ 800/465-4329
or 361/883-5731), with rates for two of $99 to $129; **La Quinta,** 5155 I-37, Exit 3A (☎ 800/687-6667 or 361/888-5721),
with rates for two of $59 to $89; **Motel 6,** 845 Lantana St.,
I-37 Exit 4B (☎ 361/289-9397), with rates for two of $38 to
$49; **Ramada Inn Bayfront,** 601 N. Water St. (☎ 800/
272-6232 or 361/882-8100), with rates for two of $69 to $89.
A reasonably priced independent motel is the **Sea Shell Inn
Motel,** 202 Kleberg Place (☎ 361/888-5291), with rates for
two of $50 to $95.

In addition to the chains listed above and the properties discussed below, **Sand Dollar Hospitality,** 3605 Mendenhall St.
(☎ 800/528-7782 or 361/853-1222; fax 361/814-1285),
arranges bed-and-breakfast stays in private homes in Corpus
Christi and the surrounding areas at rates ranging from $75 to
$150 a double per night. The homes have from one to four
bedrooms available, and all serve a full breakfast.

Room tax adds 15% to rates, and the highest rates in the
Corpus Christi area are in the summer.

Christy Estates Suites. 3942 Holly Rd., Corpus Christi, TX 78415. ☎ **800/ 678-4836** or 361/854-1091. Fax 361/854-4766. www.christyestatessuites. com. 266 suites. A/C TV TEL. $69–$139 suite; weekly and monthly rates available. AE, DC, DISC, MC, V. Pets accepted with $45 fee. No pets or children in spa suites.

This all-suite facility has one- and two-bedroom units, including 20 attractive theme suites that are a very good value compared to the area's standard motel rooms. All have full-size, fully equipped kitchens and full bathrooms with shower/tub combos. The basic suites are spacious (800 square ft.), with attractive, modern furnishings that have the feel of upscale condominium units. The spa suites are similar with the addition of large (2- to 4-person) and luxurious in-room spas with Italian tile. The 20 theme units all have spas, king-sized beds, and big-screen TVs, and are tastefully decorated in themes ranging from ancient Greece to a cave, and many have mood lighting and stereo equipment. Christy Estates has two outdoor swimming pools—one family and one adults only—plus a whirlpool tub and two self-serve Laundromats.

✪ **George Blucher House.** 211 N. Carrizo, Corpus Christi, TX 78401. ☎ **866/ 884-4884** or 361/884-4884. Fax 361/884-4885. www. georgeblucherhouse. com. 6 units. A/C TV TEL. $100–$175 double. Rates include full breakfast. Holiday and special event weekends require a minimum 2-night stay. AE, DISC, MC, V. Children over 12 accepted with prior approval.

This wonderful B&B combines the ambience of an elegant historic home with modern amenities including telephones with voice mail, TVs with VCRs, private bathrooms, and plush robes. Built in 1904 for well-to-do Corpus Christi residents George and Alice von Blucher (their descendants dropped the "von"), this 5,000 square foot home was purchased in 1999 by history buff Tracey Smith, who thoroughly researched the home's past to guarantee that the restoration would be as accurate as possible. After about a year of work, the B&B opened in June 2000, with six uniquely decorated units, each named after one of the von Blucher's children. For instance, the very feminine Pearl's Room is pink, with American and French antiques, a queen-sized bed, and a private balcony with views of downtown; and Nellie's Room is decorated in a floral motif, with American and French country furnishings and two twin beds. Most rooms are on the second floor (there is no elevator), but one ground-level unit, Jasper's Room, is wheelchair accessible.

One room has a shower only, the rest have full bathrooms with shower/tub combos. Most of the furnishings are antiques (many from the innkeeper's family), and there are some reproductions; and bed linens, towels, and the like are all top quality.

Breakfasts here are a splendid event, served by candlelight. Breakfast might include entrees such as chicken pecan quiche or eggs Benedict with artichokes, spinach, and cream cheese; and a fruit dish such as baked apple with maple syrup and pecans and wrapped in a puff pastry. Smith says that special diets can be accommodated with prior notice. Common areas include a convenience bar on the second floor landing with a refrigerator, ice machine, microwave, and coffeemaker; and the library, with a comfortable sitting area and chess, dominos, backgammon, and other games. In addition, the inn is across the street from Blucher Park, a prime bird-watching area. Smoking is not permitted inside.

✪ **Omni Corpus Christi Hotel.** 900 and 707 N. Shoreline Blvd., Corpus Christi, TX 78401. ☎ **800/843-6664** or 361/887-1600. Fax 361/887-6715. www.omnihotels.com. 821 units. A/C TV TEL. $128–$228 double; suites from $200. AE, CB, DC, DISC, MC, V. Free covered parking.

The best choice in Corpus Christi for those seeking a full service hotel, the Omni consists of two towers, Bayfront and Marina, overlooking Corpus Christi Bay. As is expected in hotels of this caliber, there is a large, attractively decorated lobby (we especially liked the large sailing ship models) where you'll find a beauty salon and a gift shop, elevators, and an abundance of meeting rooms. The spacious units are simply, but very tastefully, appointed in a classic modern-America hotel style with wallpaper and mahogany wood accents. Standard rooms have two doubles or one king bed, large working desks, a TV hidden in an armoire, plush chairs, large closets with doors, several telephones (with dataports), and irons and ironing boards. All units have private balconies. We especially like the basic king rooms, which have a convenient bedside table on each side of the bed and floor-to-ceiling windows that offer spectacular views of the Gulf, particularly from the upper floors of the 20-story Bayfront Tower. The hotel has a heated indoor/outdoor swimming pool, a fully equipped health club with a dry sauna and whirlpool, indoor racquetball courts, and an in-house massage therapist. Lighted tennis courts and a golf course are nearby (golf packages are available). In addition, it offers free scheduled airport transportation, laundry service, room service, and several restaurants including the highly rated **Republic of Texas Bar & Grill** (see "Where to Dine," below). Because this hotel gets a lot of weekday business travelers, you'll get especially good rates on weekends.

CAMPING

RVers have plenty of camping choices in the Corpus Christi area, and although many of the RV parks will accept tenters, the rates are often the same as for sites with RV hook-ups, and those in tents will be surrounded by RVs. We suggest that tenters head to nearby Padre Island National Seashore or other public lands in the area, which are discussed later in this chapter.

Among RV parks here, we recommend the well-maintained **Colonia del Rey,** 1717 Waldron Rd. (near the entrance to Padre Island), Corpus Christi, TX 78418 (☎ **800/580-2435** for reservations, or ☎ **361/937-2435;** www.gocampingamerica. com/coloniadelrey; e-mail: cldelrey@intcomm.net), which has trees, grass, a swimming pool, and all the other usual amenities, and rates of $21 to $23 for full hook-ups.

WHERE TO DINE

The favorite local fast-food burger chain is **Whataburger,** which began and remains headquartered in Corpus Christi. It has more then 20 locations in the city and over 500 more throughout Texas and the surrounding states. Whataburgers are open around the clock with similar prices but slightly better food (at least in our opinion) than the better-known national chains. And they must be doing something right— the company celebrated its 50th anniversary in 2000.

✪ **Mamma Mia's.** 128 N. Mesquite St. ☎ **361/883-3773.** Reservations not accepted. Main courses $8.75–$24.75. No credit cards. Tues–Fri 11am–2pm, Tues–Sat 5:30pm–"until." Closed 1 or 2 weeks in June. MEDITERRANEAN.

This is a really fancy place for south Texas, with white table linens and fresh flowers in an atmosphere best described as casually elegant. But what keeps the locals coming back (and back and back and back) is the food—what we perceive as the best Italian and Mediterranean cuisine in Corpus Christi. There are more than 50 items on the menu, plus five daily specials (including three fresh fish and one vegetarian). Our recommendations here include the pasta pesto alla marino—pasta in a sauce of basil, olive oil, mushrooms, broccoli, and pine nuts—and rigatoni rustica—rigatoni topped with sweet sausage, asparagus, broccoli, garlic, and olive oil. The menu also includes veal, chicken, beef, and pork. The Caesar salad (served either as a side or in a larger entree portion) is excellent.

Pier 99. 2822 N. Shoreline Blvd. ☎ **361/887-0764.** Main courses $4.95–$16.95. AE, DISC, MC, V. Sun–Thurs 9am–9pm, Fri–Sat 11am–10pm. SEAFOOD/BURGERS.

For good food at reasonable prices and a definitely upbeat atmosphere, leave your suit and tie in the car and head to Pier 99. This is a fun beach hangout where the noisy dining room has way too many neon beer signs and other items adorning the walls and ceiling. We like the less claustrophobic back deck, which offers a good view of the USS *Lexington* aircraft carrier in the harbor. The menu features fresh seafood (what else?) like the fried shrimp, fish or oyster baskets, served with fries or slaw for under $8; an all-you-can-eat fish special; and more elaborate entrees such as shrimp scampi, Cajun shrimp, boiled shrimp, and Alaskan snow crabs. There are also chicken dishes, steaks, and burgers—your choice of ½- or 1-pound. You won't leave Pier 99 hungry. There's often music on the back deck (no cover charge), which brings up one of the house rules: Don't feed the birds or band members, regardless of how hungry or cute you think they look.

Randall's Premium Deli. 600 Building, 600 Leopard St., #106. ☎ **361/884-1901.** $2.75–$5.45. AE, DC, DISC, MC, V. Mon–Fri 8am–2:30pm. DELI.

Our choice for a quick breakfast or lunch, and especially for a sandwich to go, Randall's is a simply decorated little storefront deli where you order at a counter, pick up your grub, and either sit at one of the cafe-style tables or head out to a park or beach. There are more than two dozen varieties of sandwiches, ranging from ham and cheese on your choice of bread to Philly steak to the Randall's veggie—sliced avocado, mushrooms, cucumbers, lettuce, tomato, and alfalfa sprouts on wheat toast or wrapped in pita bread. There are also more than a dozen stuffed potatoes, soups and salads, and fast food–style breakfast items.

✪ **Recio's.** 3150 S. Alameda St. ☎ **361/888-4040.** Main courses $3.75–$8.95. AE, DC, DISC, MC, V. Mon–Sat 7am–8pm; Sun 7am–2pm. MEXICAN TAQUERIA.

South Texas is littered with *taquerias*—restaurants that specialize in *taquitos* (similar to a burrito but folded), tacos, enchiladas, and other Tex-Mex and Mexican favorites—and Recio's is among the best. Locally owned and operated by Robert and Minerva Recio, this justly popular restaurant serves homemade cooked-to-order food in a pleasant, casual atmosphere. Decor is simple, with an open dining room of white walls, light wood tables, upholstered chairs, and colorful paintings by local artists. Try Rob's Parillada for Two, a platter of beef and chicken fajitas, topped with bell peppers and onions and served with ranchero beans, rice, guacamole, pico de gallo, and salad; or Recio's deluxe, a Mexican combination plate for the very hungry. Also good is that Texas staple: chicken-fried steak with gravy, served with fries and salad. The restaurant offers a variety of breakfast plates and smoked meats. Breakfast is served all day on weekends.

✪ **Republic of Texas Bar & Grill.** At the Omni Bayfront Hotel, 900 N. Shoreline Blvd. ☎ **361/886-3515.** Reservations strongly recommended. Main courses $13.95–$34.95. AE, DISC, MC, V. Mon–Sat 5:30–10:30pm, Sun 5:30–9pm. STEAK.

This is the spot to celebrate a special occasion. Located on the 20th floor of the Omni Bayfront Hotel, the Republic of Texas Bar & Grill is expensive, and worth every penny of it. There are four levels to the dining room, all with breathtaking views of the bay, with upholstered seating, light wood accents, trophy heads, ship models, and a refined, subdued atmosphere. Appetizers include the delightful, giant portobello mushroom stuffed with sweet sausage and garlic herb cheese, and all entrees are served with fresh-baked onion bread with a smoky cheddar cheese spread. This is primarily a steakhouse, and all beef is top USDA premium choice corn-fed that is hand cut and grilled over a fire of oak and mesquite. You won't be disappointed with any of the beef, but we particularly recommend the 16-ounce New York strip or the 24-ounce porterhouse. The menu usually also features several game dishes, such as mesquite-grilled quail, a chicken or pork selection, and seafood such as the wonderfully moist and flaky mesquite-grilled Pacific Northwest salmon. Sides include huge baked Idaho potatoes and garlic mashed potatoes, which are fine, but the house specialty hash browns are exquisite. There is also an extensive wine list and a good stock of microbrewed beers, as well as homemade desserts. Service is excellent.

Wallbanger's Gourmet Hamburgers. 4100 S. Staples St., Carmel Village. ☎ **361/855-8007.** Reservations not accepted. Main courses $3–$9. AE, MC, V. Mon–Thurs 11am–11pm, Fri–Sat 11am–1am. AMERICAN.

A hamburger joint with personality, Wallbanger's has the look of a Texas saloon—a big, open room, sort of dimly lit, with booths and tables and oldies music blaring away. Order at the counter and pick up your food when your number is called, and help yourself at the 50-plus-item salad bar (one of the best we've seen in these parts) or the baked potato bar. Hamburgers are the main things here, and they're made from chuck, ground fresh daily, and range from ⅓-pound to a humongous 3 pounds, the biggest we've seen anywhere. Hamburger buns are baked fresh daily. The menu also includes rib-eye steak, chicken-fried steak, grilled chicken breast, and several sandwiches.

★ **Water Street Seafood Company.** 309 N. Water St. ☎ **361/882-8683.** Reservations for large parties only. Main courses $5.95–$18. AE, DISC, MC, V. Sun–Thurs 11am–10pm, Fri–Sat 11am–11pm. Closed Thanksgiving and Christmas. SEAFOOD.

Our vote for the best seafood restaurant in Corpus Christi goes to the Water Street Seafood Company and its attached sister restaurant, the Water Street Oyster Bar, which has the same menu. The joined restaurants are decorated in a nautical motif, with a beach scene mural, fishing decor, wood tables, and a tile floor. Although there's an extensive menu, with specialties such as shrimp enchiladas—red corn tortillas stuffed with shrimp, Monterey and hot pepper jack cheeses, and topped with a homemade sauce—and a mesquite-grilled 8-ounce Angus tenderloin fillet, before even looking at the menu, those in the know check the blackboard for the daily fish specials, which can be prepared blackened, mesquite-grilled, sautéed, broiled, or fried, and are served with a salad, seasonal vegetables, and the restaurant's wonderful rice pilaf. Everything at Water Street is prepared fresh, and the staff is very accommodating about making substitutions, meeting individuals' dietary needs, or providing smaller portions (at a lower price!).

CORPUS CHRISTI AFTER DARK

For a relatively small city, Corpus Christi offers plenty to do in the evening. The **Cathedral Concert Series,** 505 N. Upper Broadway (☎ **361/888-7444**), offers six concerts each year during its October through May season, featuring both local and national performers. One is a benefit concert, and the other five are free. Recent concerts have included the Berlin Philharmonic Woodwind Quintet, Westwind Brass of San Diego, the Brazilian Guitar Quartet, the Glenn Miller Orchestra, and the Corpus Christi Symphony Orchestra. The **Corpus Christi Ballet,** 1621 N. Mesquite (☎ **361/ 882-4588;** www.tamu.edu/ccballet), presents a variety of productions from September through April, including an annual performance of *The Nutcracker,* with the Corpus Christi Symphony each December. Single tickets are priced from $10 to $35, with special children's programs costing $5.

Although certainly not in the same league with New Orleans, Corpus Christi does have a fairly active bar scene, with a number of bars and nightclubs, many with live music, on Chaparral and Water Streets. For country and Tejano dance music, try **La Playa** at 417 Chaparral St. (☎ **361/882-1664**); and you'll also find a variety of live music at **Dr. Rockits Blues Bar,** 709 Chaparral St. (☎ **361/884-7634**), **Tom Foolery's Chill & Grill,** 301 Chaparral St. (☎ **361/887-0029**), and **Executive Surf Club,** 309 Water St. (☎ **361/884-7873**). There's also live music and a somewhat rowdy beach hangout scene at **Pier 99,** 2822 N. Shoreline Blvd. (☎ **361/ 887-0764**), described above under "Where to Dine." You'll find a more subdued crowd at the piano bar at **Harry O'Brien's,** 304 Chaparral St. (☎ **361/882-2192**).

2 Padre Island National Seashore

37 miles SE of Corpus Christi

Some 70 miles of delightful, white-sand beach, picturesque sand dunes, and warm ocean waters make Padre Island National Seashore a favorite year-round playground along the Texas Gulf Coast. One of the longest stretches of undeveloped coastline in America, this National Park Service–managed property is an ideal spot for swimming, sunbathing, fishing, beachcombing, windsurfing, camping, and four-wheeling, and also offers excellent bird-watching opportunities and a chance to see several species of rare sea turtles. The island was named for Padre José Nicolás Balli, a Mexican priest, who in 1804 founded a mission, settlement, and ranch about 26 miles north of the island's southernmost tip.

Padre Island is a barrier island, essentially a sand bar that helps protect the mainland from the full force of ocean storms. Like other barrier islands, one of the constants of Padre Island is change; wind and waves relentlessly shape and recreate the island, as grasses and other hardy plants strive to get a foothold in the shifting sands. ✪ **Padre Island's Gulf side,** with miles of beach accessible only to those with four-wheel-drive vehicles, offers wonderful surf fishing; while the channel between the island and mainland—the Laguna Madre—offers excellent windsurfing and a protected area for small power boats and sailboats.

ESSENTIALS
GETTING THERE

From Corpus Christi take Tex. 358 (South Padre Island Drive) southeast across the JFK Causeway to Padre Island, and follow Park Road 22 south to the national seashore.

VISITOR INFORMATION

For information contact **Padre Island National Seashore,** P.O. Box 181300, Corpus Christi, TX 78480-1300 (☎ **361/ 949-8068;** www.nps.gov/pais). The Park Service also maintains a recorded beach and road condition information line (☎ **361/949-8175**). The visitor center complex, along Park Road 22 at Malaquite Beach, has an observation deck, a bookstore, and a variety of exhibits on the human history of Padre Island and its flora and fauna, especially the endangered Kemp's ridley sea turtle. In the same complex are a concessionaire-operated snack bar and a store (☎ **361/949-9368;** www.foreverresorts.com) that sells camping and fishing supplies and gift items, and rents chairs, umbrellas, body boards, and other beach toys and equipment. The visitor center is open from 8:30am to 6pm from June through Labor Day weekend, and from 8:30am to 4:30pm the rest of the year (closed Christmas and New Year's Day), and the snack bar and store are usually open similar hours. The park is open 24 hours a day.

Located at Bird Island Basin, **Worldwinds Windsurfing** (☎ **361/949-7472**) offers rentals and sales of sailboards and wetsuits, plus windsurfing lessons during the summer. Call for current fees and schedule.

Fees & Regulations

Entry for up to 7 days costs $10 per vehicle, or $5 per individual on foot or bike. There is also a $5 day-use fee at Bird Island Basin. Regulations here are much like those at other National Park Service properties, which essentially require that visitors not disturb wildlife or damage the site's natural features and facilities. Pets must be leashed and are not permitted on the swimming beach in front of the visitor center. Although driving off road is permitted on some sections of beach, the dunes, grasslands, and tidal flats are closed to all vehicles. Loaded firearms, fireworks, nudity, and the possession or use of metal detectors are also prohibited.

When to Go

Summer is the busiest time here, although it is generally hot (highs in the 90s) and very humid. Sea breezes in late afternoon and evening help moderate the heat. Winters are generally mild, with highs from the 50s to the 70s, and lows in the 40s and 50s. Only occasionally does the temperature drop below 40°F, and a freeze is extremely rare. Hurricane season, from June through October, is the rainiest time of the year and also has the highest surf. Our favorite months to visit Padre Island are November and December, when it is still usually warm enough for swimming, but not nearly as hot or crowded as summer.

Safety

Swimmers are advised to never swim alone, and swimmers and those walking barefoot on the beach should watch out for the Portuguese man-of-war, a blue jellyfish that can cause a painful sting. There are also poisonous rattlesnakes in the dunes, grasslands, and mud flats; and hazardous materials, such as medical waste and containers of possibly dangerous chemicals, occasionally wash up on the beach.

Ranger Programs

A variety of **interpretive programs** are held year-round, ranging from guided beach or birding walks to talks outside the visitor center to evening campground campfire programs. These programs usually last from 30 to 45 minutes and cover subjects such as migrating or resident birds, seashells, the island's plant life or animals, the human history of the island, or things that wash up on the beach. Padre Island also has a **Junior Ranger Program** for children 5 to 13. Kids answer questions in a free booklet and talk with rangers about the national seashore to earn certificates, Junior Ranger badges, and sea turtle stickers.

EXPLORING THE HIGHLIGHTS BY CAR

Padre Island National Seashore has an 8.5-mile paved road that leads to the visitor center complex. In addition, most of the beaches are open to licensed, street-legal motor vehicles; some sections have hard-packed sand that makes an adequate roadbed for two-wheel drive vehicles while most of the beach requires four-wheel-drive. See "Sports & Outdoor Pursuits: Four-Wheeling," below.

SPORTS & OUTDOOR PURSUITS

BEACHCOMBING   The best times for beachcombing are usually early mornings, and especially immediately after a storm when you're apt to find a variety of seashells, seaweed, driftwood, and the like. These types of items can be collected, but live animals and historical or archaeological objects should be left alone. Among shells sometimes found at Padre Island, you'll find lightning whelks, moon snails, Scotch bonnets, Atlantic cockles, bay scallops, and sand dollars. The best shell hunting is often in winter, when storms disturb the water and thrust shells ashore; and many of the best shells are often found on Little Shell and Big Shell beaches, accessible only to those with four-wheel-drive vehicles. Metal detectors are not permitted on the beach.

BIRD WATCHING & WILDLIFE VIEWING   More than 350 species of birds frequent Padre Island, and every visitor is bound to see and hear at least some of them. The island is a key stopping point for a variety of migratory species traveling between North and Central America, making spring and fall especially good times for bird watching. And, since a number of species don't get any farther south than Padre Island, winter also provides ample birding opportunities. Additionally, the area is the northern boundary of a number of species usually found in Central America, such as green jays and jacanas.

Birding here is very easy, especially for those with four-wheel-drive vehicles who can drive slowly down the more remote stretches of beach. Experienced bird watchers say it is best to remain in your vehicle because humans on foot scare off birds sooner than approaching vehicles. As would be expected by its name, Bird Island Basin is also a good choice for birders as long as the marshes have water. The most commonly observed bird is the laughing gull, which is a year-round resident. Other species to watch for include rare brown pelicans plus the more common American white pelicans, long-billed curlews, great blue herons, sandhill cranes, ruddy turnstones, Caspian and Royal terns, willets, Harris' hawks, reddish egrets, northern bobwhites, mourning doves, horned larks, great-tailed grackles, and red-winged blackbirds.

In addition to birds, the island is also home to the spotted ground squirrel, which is often seen in the dunes near the visitor center, white-tailed deer, coyotes, black-tailed jackrabbits, lizards, a number of non-poisonous snakes, and the poisonous western diamondback rattlesnake and western massasauga.

BOATING   A boat ramp is located at Bird Island Basin, which provides access to Laguna Madre, a protected bay that is ideal for small power and sailboats. Boat launching is not permitted on the Gulf side of the island. Personal watercraft are not permitted in Laguna Madre (except to get from the boat ramp to open water outside the park boundaries) but are allowed on the Gulf side beyond the 5-mile marker.

FISHING   Fishing is popular year-round. Surf fishing is permitted everywhere along the Gulf side, except at Malaquite Beach, and yields whiting, redfish, black drum, and speckled sea trout; while anglers in Laguna Madre catch flounder, sheepshead, and croaker. A Texas fishing license with a saltwater stamp is required. Licenses, along with copies of current fishing regulations and some fishing supplies, are available at a concessionaire-operated store (see "Visitor Information," above).

FOUR-WHEELING   Licensed and street-legal motor vehicles (but not ATVs) are permitted on most of the beach at Padre Island National Seashore (but not Malaquite Beach or the fragile dunes, grasslands, and tidal flats). Most standard passenger vehicles can make it down the first 5 miles of South Beach, but those planning to drive further south down the island (another 55 miles are open to motor vehicles) will need four-wheel-drive vehicles. Markers are located every 5 miles, and those driving down the beach are advised to watch for soft

The Race to Save the Sea Turtles

The Gulf of Mexico is home to five species of sea turtles, all of which are either endangered or threatened, including the Kemp's ridley, considered to be the most endangered sea turtle in the world, with only about 3,000 in existence. Kemp's ridleys have almost circular shells, grow to about 2 feet long, and weigh about 100 pounds. Adults are olive green on top and yellow below, and their main food source is crabs. Their main nesting area, historically, is along a 16-mile stretch of beach at Playa de Rancho Nuevo in Tamaulipas, Mexico, and although females lay about 100 eggs at a time, only about 1% of the hatchlings survives to adulthood.

In the 1970s, an international effort was begun to establish a second nesting area at Padre Island National Seashore, using the theory that sea turtles always return to the beach where they were hatched to lay their eggs. More than 22,000 eggs were gathered from Playa de Rancho Nuevo between 1978 and 1988, placed in boxes containing Padre Island sand, and shipped to Texas where they were placed in incubators. After hatching, about 13,500 baby turtles were released on the beach at Padre Island National Seashore and allowed to crawl into the water for a quick swim. Fearing that the young turtles would become lunch for predators, National Park Service biologists captured them and sent them to a marine fisheries lab in Galveston, where they spent up to a year growing big enough to have a better chance of survival in the wild. They were then tagged and released into the Gulf of Mexico.

Since then some of the turtles have returned to Padre Island and other sections of the Texas Gulf Coast to nest, and Park Service workers have collected a number of eggs for incubation and eventual release. The eggs are collected in late spring and summer, and anyone seeing a nesting sea turtle is asked to not disturb it but to report its location to national seashore personnel. The public can attend releases of the hatchlings, which usually occur in June and August; for information on release dates call the **Hatchling Hotline** at ☎ **361/949-7163.**

sand and high water, and to carry a shovel, jack, boards, and other emergency equipment. In addition, we suggest that those planning their first 4×4 trip at Padre Island talk with rangers first about current conditions and what they will encounter. Unless otherwise posted, the speed limit on the beach is 15 miles per hour. Northbound vehicles have the right of way.

HIKING The national seashore has miles and miles of beach that are ideal for walking and hiking, although plodding through sand and surf can be very tiring. There's also the paved and fairly easy **Grasslands Nature Trail,** a ¾-mile self-guided loop trail that meanders through grass-covered areas of sand dunes. Numbered posts along the trail correspond with descriptions of plants and other aspects of the natural landscape in a free brochure available at the trailhead or the visitor center. You'll need insect repellent to combat mosquitoes, and, because western diamondback rattlesnakes also inhabit the area, it is best to stay on the trail and watch where you put your feet and hands.

SWIMMING & SURFING Warm air and water temperatures make swimming practically a year-round activity here—January through March are really the only time it's too chilly—and swimming is permitted along the entire beach. The most popular swimming area is 4.5-mile-long Malaquite Beach, also called Closed Beach, which is closed to motor vehicles. There are lifeguards stationed only at Malaquite Beach, and only in summer, and a concessionaire operates a snack bar, store, and rental facility (see "Visitor Information," above). Although waves at Padre Island are not of the Hawaii or California size, they're often sufficient for surfing, which is permitted in most areas, but not at Malaquite Beach.

WINDSURFING The Bird Island Basin area on Laguna Madre is considered one of America's best spots for windsurfing because of its warm water, shallow depth, and consistent, steady winds. During the summer, a concessionaire rents and sells windsurfing equipment and offers lessons (see "Visitor Information," above).

Tip for Travelers with Disabilities

Specially designed fat-tire wheelchairs for use in the sand, and even in the water, are available at no charge at the visitor center. They do require someone to push.

What in the World Is Red Tide?

Up and down the Gulf Coast you'll hear about, and sometimes see, what is called "red tide," which sounds a lot scarier than the phenomenon really is. Red tide appears to be one of the few environmental problems that we probably can't blame on human beings. It's a naturally occurring situation in which a higher than usual concentration of a type of algae called *Gymnodinium breve* occurs, resulting in discoloration of the ocean water that usually produces red patches on the water surface. The bad part is that this alga produces a toxin that paralyzes fish, including their ability to breathe, so the fish die and often wash up on Gulf Coast beaches such as Padre Island.

The Texas Department of Health says that it is usually safe to eat fish, crabs, and shrimp during a red tide infestation (although not ones found sick or dead, since you wouldn't know what affected them); but you should not eat oysters, clams, or other bivalve mollusks from red tide water because you could get neurotoxic shellfish poisoning, which is not fatal but can cause severe nausea and dizziness. In addition, the red tide alga in the ocean water, and even in ocean spray, has been known to irritate the lungs, nose, and throat of some people. The good news is that red tides are usually isolated patches that don't effect an entire beach, and usually do not remain in any location very long.

CAMPING

Padre Island National Seashore's developed **Malaquite Campground,** about ½-mile north of the visitor center, has 47 sites ($8 per night) that are available on a first-come first-served basis year-round. Sites are within 100 feet of the beach with good views of the Gulf, and the campground has cold showers, restrooms, and picnic tables. There are no RV hook-ups, but there is a dump station. There's also a campfire circle where evening ranger programs are presented year-round.

The primitive **Yarborough Pass Campground,** located on the Laguna Madre 15½ miles south of the visitor center, is accessible only with a four-wheel-drive vehicle. It's open year-round, but has no facilities, and no fee is charged. Get directions from the visitor center before setting out. In addition, free primitive camping is permitted on the Gulf beaches and at Bird Island Basin.

WHERE TO STAY & DINE

The closest lodging and dining is in Corpus Christi, which is discussed in the previous section of this chapter.

3 South Padre Island

366 miles SW of Houston

South Padre Island is truly a resort town, with about 3,000 year-round residents, and an influx of several thousand more when the winter chill sends northerners south in search of sunshine and warmth. Water sports are a major draw, from power boating, sailing, and windsurfing to bay, surf, and deep-sea fishing. And some of us simply want to relax on the beach, allowing the gentle murmur of the water to soothe our senses and wash away the stress of our hectic modern world. More energetic visitors can also bicycle, play tennis and golf, and go horseback riding. Birding is as popular here as in other areas of south Texas, with more than 300 species.

A wide variety of lodgings are available, from beach houses to condominiums, small hotels to bed-and-breakfasts to full-service resorts. The sunsets are grand, reflecting in the water of the Laguna Madre, and many restaurants capitalize on their location with outdoor seating. Ready your taste buds to enjoy fresh seafood of all kinds prepared in a variety of seasonings—continental to Mexican, broiled to deep fried. And, if you catch your own, some restaurants will be happy to cook it for you!

Incorporated in 1973, South Padre Island stretches along 25 miles of sand on the southern tip of Padre Island just across the Laguna Madre from the mainland and the small town of Port Isabel. Easily accessible by plane into nearby cities, it has become a favored place for conventions. But don't bring your business suits—South Padre Island takes its role of laid-back vacation spot seriously, and ties are expressly forbidden.

ESSENTIALS
GETTING THERE

From U.S. 77/83, which connects to Harlingen, McAllen, and Corpus Christi, take Tex. 100 east to Port Isabel and then across the Queen Isabella Causeway to the south end of South Padre Island. From Brownsville, take Tex. 48 northeast to Tex. 100.

SOUTH PADRE ISLAND PROCLAMATION

WHEREAS, South Padre Island is a subtropical vacation and meeting destination for hundreds of thousands of people each year; and

WHEREAS, Visitors come across the Laguna Madre bay to the island to escape the workday world, refocusing their priorities on our beautiful white sandy beaches along the Gulf of Mexico, the unequaled recreational opportunities, fresh-caught seafood, game fishing, birding and nature trails, and all of the informal ambience anyone could ever desire for a vacation or for the site of an island convention; and

WHEREAS, Because this pristine atmosphere is sometimes shattered by the appearance of the most blatant symbol of conformity and business throughout the world—the "tie"—it has become necessary to further protect our visitors and citizens. Ties have been spotted in hotel lobbies, along Padre Boulevard, and even poolside at some of our most exotic resorts. The very appearance of a tie causes a discordant note for our visitors, sometimes causing serious regression back to their humdrum and ordinary business lives.

NOW, THEREFORE, be it proclaimed by the Board of Aldermen of the Town of South Padre Island, Texas, the "tie" is detrimental to the welfare of South Padre Island and its visitors and is hereby banished from our land and waters forever. A written warning notice will be issued to first offenders by the South Padre Island Police Department. This warning notice will be accompanied by a complimentary South Padre Island T-Shirt to assist such offenders in adjusting to the correct attire and lifestyles of the island. Second offenders will be fined the amount of a fine silk tie and the offending tie will be confiscated and destroyed.

IN WITNESS THEREOF, I have set my hand and caused the seal of the Town of South Padre Island, Texas, to be affixed this the 4th day of June, 1997.

Edmund K. Cyganiewicz, Mayor

Attested by Joyce Adams, City Secretary

The closest airport is the **Brownsville/South Padre Island International Airport** (☎ 956/542-4373) at Brownsville (about 28 miles southwest), which is served by Continental (☎ 800/425-0280), Continental Express (☎ 800/523-3273),

American Eagle (☎ **800/761-4343**), Southwest Airlines (☎ **800/435-9792**), and Sun Country (☎ **800/752-1218**) fly into **Valley International Airport** (☎ **956/430-8600**) in Harlingen, about 40 miles west.

VISITOR INFORMATION

Contact the **South Padre Island Convention and Visitors Bureau,** 600 Padre Blvd., South Padre Island, TX 78597 (☎ **800/SOPADRE** or 956/761-3005; fax 956/761-3024; www.sopadre.com). There's an excellent **visitor center** (☎ **956/761-6433**) at 600 Padre Blvd., on the right shortly after you exit the causeway and turn north onto Padre Boulevard.

GETTING AROUND

Padre Boulevard is the main drag along the island and runs north-south. Parallel to it are Laguna Boulevard 1 block west and Gulf Boulevard on the east side of the island, facing the Gulf of Mexico.

South Padre Island operates **"The Wave"** (☎ **856/761-1025**), a free shuttle, between Port Isabel and the South Padre Island Convention Centre, daily between 7am and 7pm. It does not run between noon and 1pm, nor does it cross the causeway during high winds or for the 9am and 3pm stops. "The Wave" leaves from the Sea Ranch Restaurant on the hour, heads north on Padre and Gulf Boulevards, making several stops, reaching the Convention Centre about 20 minutes after the hour. It then turns south on Padre Boulevard, stopping along the way, then crossing the Causeway to Port Isabel, reaching the Lighthouse about 40 minutes after the hour. After two more stops it returns to its beginning point.

FAST FACTS

Health services are available at **Balley Regional Island Clinic,** 3000 Padre Blvd. The **post office,** 4705 Padre Blvd., is open Monday through Friday from 8am to 4pm, Saturday from 10am to noon.

SPECIAL EVENTS

The **Taste of the Island & Expo** is held in late January; the **South Padre Island Easter Egg Hunt** takes place on Easter Sunday; the **Windsurfing Blowout** is held from late April to early May; the **Shrimp on the Barbie Cook-Off** takes place in May; the **Beach Volleyball Classic** is held on Memorial Day and Labor Day weekends; the **Windjammer Regatta** is in July; the **Beachcomber's Art Show** takes place in late July; the **Texas International Fishing Tournament (TIFT)** is held from late July into early August; the **Longest Causeway Run & Wellness Walk** takes place during early October; the **World's Championship Shrimp Cook-Off** is staged in mid-October; the **South Padre Island Kite Festival** is held in early November; the **Lighting of the Island and the Christmas Tree** takes place in late November; and the **Island of Lights Street Parade** is held in December.

WHAT TO SEE & DO

Except where noted, the following attractions are located on South Padre Island.

The Port Isabel Historical Museum. 317 E. Railroad Ave., Port Isabel. ☎ 956/943-7602. www.panam.edu/dept/csl/pih_museum.html. Admission $3 adults, $2 seniors 55 and over, $1 students, 50¢ children ages 3–5, free for children under 3. Tues–Sat 10am–4pm, Sun 1–4pm. Located 2 blocks from the Port Isabel Lighthouse at the corner of Railroad Ave. and Tarnava St.

This restored 1899 Victorian commercial building houses a delightful, small-town museum dedicated to describing the history of the area from the time it was a supply depot during the Mexican-American War, through the Civil War and the area's development as a shrimping and fishing capital, to today's recreation industry. There are interactive exhibits, a large display of Mexican-American War artifacts, a 1906 Victor Morales "Fish Mural," plus a theater and gift shop. Also on the grounds is a water well, dating from the Mexican-American War when Zachary Taylor's troops were quartered here.

Port Isabel Lighthouse State Historical Park. 421 E. Queen Isabel Blvd. in Lighthouse Square, at the west end of the Queen Isabella Causeway, Port Isabel. ☎ 956/943-1172. www.tpwd.state.tx.us. Admission to grounds, free; tour $2 adults, $1 students. Wed–Sun 10am–noon, 1–4pm. Closed some holidays.

This 1852 lighthouse, which helped guide ships through Brazos Santiago Pass to Point Isabel until 1905, now affords panoramic views of Port Isabel, South Padre Island, and as far as the eye can see out over the Gulf of Mexico. Also on Lighthouse Square, is a recently constructed replica of the lighthouse keeper's cottage, copied from the 1850 blueprints for the original. The lighthouse and cottage are part of a $2.5 million restoration project currently underway.

Sea Turtle, Inc. 6617 Padre Blvd. ☎ **956/761-1720.** www.seaturtleinc. com. E-mail: ridley97@aol.com. Admission $2 adults, $1 children ages 5–12, free for children 4 and under. Tues–Wed, Fri–Sun 10am–4pm.

Each of the seven worldwide species of sea turtles are either threatened or endangered, and five species are found in the Gulf of Mexico. Sea Turtle, Inc. was founded in 1977 by Ila Loetscher, affectionately dubbed the "Turtle Lady," for the main purpose of protecting and preserving the most endangered species, Kemp's ridley. The organization supports conservation and rehabilitation of all marine turtles. Volunteer presentations with live sea turtles, Tuesdays and Saturdays at 10am, will help you identify the different species and explain how each of us can help protect them.

Whaling Wall. South Padre Island Convention Centre, 7355 Padre Blvd. Free admission. Daily 24 hours.

This magnificent large mural, entitled "Orcas of the Gulf of Mexico," envelops a building next to the Laguna Madre Nature Trail at the South Padre Island Convention & Visitors Bureau. Internationally known environmental artist Wyland chose South Padre Island for his 53rd mural (the only one in Texas). Plans call for 100 Whaling Walls to help educate people on the importance of marine conservation.

SPORTS & OUTDOOR PURSUITS

BIRD WATCHING   More than 300 species of birds make South Padre Island their home during part or most of every year. The **Laguna Madre Nature Trail,** adjacent to the South Padre Island Convention Centre at the north end of town, is a boardwalk that meanders out over the wetlands of the Laguna Madre and around a fresh water pond. There are a few blinds where you can set up a scope and sit for hours unseen by the birds. Some of the birds you might watch for are egrets, herons, oystercatchers, rails, soras, kingfishers, moorhens, terns, and the white-phase reddish egret. The boardwalk is wheelchair accessible and open 24 hours, free of charge.

FISHING   There have been record-setting catches made in the waters around South Padre Island: The state record blue marlin, at 876.5 pounds, was taken offshore.

The beach and jetties are easily accessible and very popular with "winter Texans," retired residents of the northern United States and Canada who spend at least part of the winter in the south Texas warmth. There are numerous local charter captains specializing in offshore big game fishing, where anglers try for blue marlin, white marlin, sailfish, swordfish, wahoo, tuna, and mako shark. Offshore fishing also includes red drum, spotted sea trout, snapper, grouper, tarpon, and king mackerel.

The Laguna Madre, on average only 2 feet deep, is perfect for world-class light-tackle sport fishing. The lush carpet of sea grasses on its bottom provides good habitat and food for red drum, spotted sea trout, flounder, black drum, and snook, and locals brag that there are more of these fish per acre than in any other bay on the Texas Gulf.

The Texas International Fishing Tournament (TIFT) has been going strong for more than 60 years and attracts more than 1,000 participants each July. The 5-day event includes bay, offshore, and tarpon fishing divisions, and is open to anglers of all ages.

GOLF   The **South Padre Island Golf Club,** 1 Golf House Rd., Laguna Vista (☎ **956/943-5678**), is on the mainland, about 2 miles north of Port Isabel off FM 510. It is a par 72, 18-hole course, with fees of $41 to $60 for 18 holes including cart rental.

HORSEBACK RIDING   If you've always wanted to ride on the beach to the sound of breaking waves, this is the place: **Island Equestrian Center, Inc.,** P.O. Box 3633, South Padre Island, TX 78597 (☎ **956/761-4677;** www.horsesonthebeach. com). You don't have to be an accomplished equestrian to ride—in fact horses are available for all levels of riders, and they actually specialize in working with first-timers and children. There are even ponies for children under 6. This is not a trail ride, but a group ride, over miles of beautiful beach with an accompanying guide to help novices. Rides start at $25 for one hour, $30 for 1½ hours. Call for schedule and reservations.

SUNBATHING & SWIMMING   The beaches of South Padre Island are some of the best on the Gulf: The sand is fine and white, and the water is warm and shallow. In town, there are 23 access points with free parking, plus the county has a park at each end of town, with a $4 all-day parking fee, good at both parks. The nicest and most popular stretch of beach is between the Radisson and Holiday Inn. Incidentally, although lined with hotels and condos, the shoreline and adjacent beaches are public and open to everyone.

WINDSURFING   With winds averaging 14 to 17 miles per hour year-round, these waters are ideal for windsurfing. Spring and fall is the quietest, with the most beautiful weather. Hurricane season runs from August to early November, but is not often a serious problem.

WHERE TO STAY
HOTELS, MOTELS, & BED AND BREAKFASTS

Room rates vary widely in South Padre Island over the course of the year, with the lowest rates generally being in winter. Among the national chain motels in South Padre Island are **Days Inn South Padre Island,** 3913 Padre Blvd. (☎ **800/329-7466** or 956/761-7831), with rates of $59 to $189 double; **Holiday Inn SunSpree Resort,** 100 Padre Blvd. (☎ **800/531-7405** or 956/761-5401), with rates of $180 double; **Motel 6,** 4013 Padre Blvd. (☎ **800/466-8356** or 956/761-7911), with rates of $39 to $50 double; **Ramada Limited,** 4109 Padre Blvd. (☎ **800/272-6232** or 956/761-4097), with rates of $55 to $200 double; and **Super 8,** 4205 Padre Blvd. (☎ **800/800-8000** or 956/761-6300), with rates of $39 to $200 double. Room tax adds about 13% to all bills.

Brown Pelican Inn—A Bayside Bed & Breakfast. 207 W. Aries Dr., P.O. Box 2667, South Padre Island, TX 78597. ☎ **956/761-2722.** Fax 956/761-8683. www.brownpelican.com. E-mail: innkeeper@brownpelican.com. 8 units. A/C TV. $80–$120 double. Rates include continental breakfast. AE, DISC, MC, V. Not suitable for children under 12. Reservations required. From Padre Blvd., turn west onto Aries Dr. to the end. The Brown Pelican will be on your left, across from Scampi's restaurant (see "Where to Dine," below).

This deceptively simple two-story beach house with wraparound porches on both floors is an elegant and sumptuously peaceful inn. Each room is individually decorated with American and English antiques and collectibles, and finished in muted colors. Two rooms are downstairs: The Big Thicket faces the bay and has a king bed and private entrance from the porch, and the Hill Country is fully handicap accessible and has a queen bed. The upstairs rooms all have queen beds, and two face the bay, affording front-seat views of stunning sunsets over the Laguna Madre. Each room has a private bathroom, seven have showers only, and one has a tub/shower combo. There are rocking chairs on the porches that invite you to sit back and relax, and allow the gentle Gulf breezes to gently caress your face. Enjoy the homemade breakfast on the bayside porch or in the great room—freshly baked pastries, homemade granola, fresh fruit and juices, and gourmet coffee and tea. Cookies, fruit, and drinks are available in the afternoons and evenings. Smoking is allowed outside only.

☀ **Casa de Siesta Bed & Breakfast.** 4610 Padre Blvd., South Padre Island, TX 78597. ☎ **956/761-5656.** Fax 956/761-1313. www.casadesiesta.com. 12 units. A/C TV TEL. Nov–Jan $99 double; Mar, June–Aug $150 double; rest of year $125 double. Rates include continental breakfast. AE, DISC, MC, V. Pets accepted. Not suitable for children under 12.

Although located right on the main drag, the hacienda-style design of this B&B provides privacy and quiet. All the rooms open onto a portal, lined with large planters, that surrounds the attractive central patio with a fountain and swimming pool. The rooms are huge, with a dressing room and private bathroom that has a step-in shower. Each room has robes, small refrigerators, and either a king or two double beds. There are large stained-glass windows, colorful Mexican tile, rustic and solid wood furniture from Mexico, Saltillo tile floors, high ceilings, and ceiling fans. The doors are magnificent: 8 feet high, custom-made wood with rounded tops. Smoking outside only.

☀ **Radisson Resort South Padre Island.** 500 Padre Blvd., South Padre Island, TX 78597. ☎ **800/333-3333** or 956/761-6511. Fax 956/761-1602. www.radissonspi.com. E-mail: radspisales@aol.com. 188 units. A/C TV TEL. $100–$200 double, $205–$380 suite. AE, CB, DC, DISC, MC, V.

Two Catalina macaws greet visitors to this Radisson: Rad and General. They appear quite at home, surrounded as they are, with tropical plants in the high-ceilinged lobby. The landscaping around the pools is lovely: plenty of palm trees, flowers, and grass. The popular public beach just outside the hotel is the nicest in town—they rake it twice daily. The cabanas—the standard rooms—have either two double beds or one king, tub/shower combos, and are colorfully decorated with floral bedspreads and artwork with a fish motif. Those with beach views are the best, and those with oceanfront views are the most expensive.

There are two pools, three whirlpool tubs, four outdoor lighted tennis courts, a large, impressive gift shop, a restaurant that serves all three meals daily and has a big-screen TV for sporting events, and 11,000 square feet of conference space to accommodate 1,000 people. The suites, actually two-bedroom condos, are large, handsomely appointed units with sleeping for up to six, two full bathrooms, a full kitchen, and a spacious living/dining room.

Yacht Club Hotel. 700 Yturria St., Port Isabel, TX 78578. ☎ **956/ 943-1301.** Fax 956/943-2330. 23 units. A/C TV TEL. Summer and Mar $70–$75 double, $110 suite; lower off-season, highest weekends. Rates include continental breakfast. AE, MC, V.

The two-story, red-tile roofed, white-stuccoed Spanish architecture building declares its historical roots, while the lushness of the grounds affirms the present comfort and attention to visitors' needs. In the late 1920s, the Yacht Club was a private gathering place for the elite of the Rio Grande Valley and indeed the entire United States; Charles Lindbergh and other notable public figures were wont to visit. But, in 1947, the public was welcomed to its hotel, restaurant, and lounge. The ambience of the 1920s remains—right down to the small lobby and uneven stairs—but modern comforts have been added to the variety of guest rooms. As in many older properties, the rooms vary in shape and size, though none are large, but they're decorated in a Mexican motif including carved wood furniture and Mexican tile and tinwork. The suites, which have a separate sitting area with TV, are in a separate building and generally have white wicker furniture. All rooms overlook water, either the inlet or the marina. The small standard rooms have a double bed and accommodate no more than two people; suites can accommodate up to four. There's a lovely pool set among banana trees and other tropical flowering plants, and a restaurant (see "Where to Dine," below).

CAMPING

Isla Blanca Park (☎ **956/761-5493**), on the southern tip of South Padre Island, is part of the Cameron County Park System (P.O. Box 2106, South Padre Island, TX 78597). There are 600 paved sites, many of which are pull-through, and more than half have full RV hook-ups. The park also offers restrooms with showers, dump station, beach, fishing jetty, boat ramp and marina, playground, a bike trail, and beach pavilions with concessions. There is a primitive tent area right on the Laguna Madre. Rates are $10 to $20.

Destination South Padre RV Resort (☎ **800/867-2373**) is just ⅓-mile south of the Queen Isabella Causeway on

Padre Blvd. It offers 190 gravel sites with full hook-ups, rest-rooms with showers, guest laundry, and security. There's a heated pool, spa, boat dock, rec hall and game room, and planned activities. Rates are $23 to $37. There are pet restrictions, and tents are not allowed.

WHERE TO DINE

✪ **Padre Island Brewing Company.** 3400 Padre Blvd. at Bahama St. ☎ **956/761-9585.** Main courses $5.25–$18.95, salads $3–$9. AE, MC, V. Tues–Sun 11:30am–10:30pm, Mon 5–10:30pm. BREWPUB/PIZZA.

This two-story white stucco building boasts al fresco dining on the second-story deck, which offers terrific views. The fare is good brewpub: burgers cooked to order and sandwiches such as a chicken fajita, served on a French roll. Entrees include steaks, pork chops, baby back ribs, Texas quail, stuffed chicken breast, breaded beer batter shrimp, crab-stuffed flounder, and fillet of snapper. All are served with their delicious fresh-baked crusty bread, soup or salad, fresh vegetables, and your choice of garlic mashed potatoes, french fries, or herb-roasted potatoes.

The inside decor is simple, with a few chile ristras and bright posterlike paintings of different beers on the walls and rattan shades on the windows. Wheat, malt, and hopsacks cover the ceiling. Tables are wooden, some tall with bar stools, others with small Windsor-style chairs. As in most brewpubs, the brewing vats are ranged behind the bar, and visible from the front parking lot through tall windows.

Pirate's Landing. 110 N. Garcia on the water, Port Isabel. ☎ **956/943-3663.** Reservations required for dinner in summer. Main courses $5.50–$12. AE, DISC, MC, V. Sun–Thurs 11:30am–9pm, Fri–Sat 11:30am–10pm. SEAFOOD.

This distinctly nautical restaurant has several stupendous ship's models, thick ropes linking fat posts, just like on a dock, neon beer signs, and a wonderful mural of pirates (what else?) landing on shore. Seafood is prepared every way imaginable: broiled, grilled, or blackened, then maybe tossed in a salad or with pasta; dipped in a light batter and fried cholesterol-free; or, maybe, served simply with tartar sauce or as a sandwich on their homemade bread. There are also a number of non-seafood sandwiches such as Southwest Chicken, charcoal-grilled chicken breast, ham with Swiss cheese and salsa, the Border Burger, a half-pound handmade burger with Monterey

Jack and cheddar cheeses and salsa; and the Melt-Down, hot ham or turkey with American or Swiss cheese. There are also daily lunch specials.

Scampi's. 206 W. Aries. ☎ **956/761-1755.** Reservations suggested. Main courses $13.95–$24.95. AE, MC, V. Apr–Oct Sun–Thurs 6–10pm, Fri–Sat 6–11pm; Nov–Mar Sun–Thurs 5–9pm, Fri–Sat 5–11pm; bar year-round Sun–Thurs 4:30pm–12am, Fri–Sat 4:30pm–1am. From Padre Blvd., turn west onto Aries and drive to the end. Scampi's will be on your right. SEAFOOD.

Scampi's is one of the most elegant restaurants on the island, with white linen tablecloths, blue-and-white chairs, and floral photographs on the walls. The food is upscale also, with some unique offerings. Try the Peanut Butter Shrimp, prepared with garlic, ginger, soy sauce, sugar, peanut butter, and a touch of jalapeño, served with a rice pilaf; Shrimp Italiano, jumbo Gulf shrimp in olive oil, white wine, butter, garlic, and capers; or the simpler broiled, blackened, or grilled Gulf red snapper. The menu also offers filet mignon, rib-eye steak, veal, lamb, an Oriental stir-fry, Chinese vegetable salad, and several pasta dishes. There's patio dining overlooking the Laguna Madre and a fine wine list.

✪ **Ted's Restaurant.** 5717 Padre Blvd. ☎ **956/761-5327.** Reservations. Main courses $3.25–$5.75. AE, DISC, MC, V ($10 minimum for credit cards). Daily 7am–3pm. AMERICAN.

This small, very casual restaurant offers good food at reasonable prices, and the entire menu is available at all times. There are about a dozen Formica-topped tables, Roman shades on the windows, and hanging plants scattered about. Although small, the room is light and airy, and the service is prompt, with coffee cups being frequently refilled. Food is cooked to order though, so don't be impatient. Breakfast includes the usual eggs, pancakes, and waffles, plus a breakfast taco, *migas* (two eggs scrambled with onions, tomato, and corn tortilla, garnished with cheese and served with refried beans, salsa, and tortillas), and huevos rancheros. Our choice for lunch is beef or chicken fajitas with flour tortillas, picante sauce, refried beans and several optional toppings like jalapeños, guacamole, or sour cream. Also offered are burgers, sandwiches, and salads. Be sure to check the blackboard for the daily specials.

Yacht Club Restaurant. In the Yacht Club Hotel, Port Isabel. ☎ **956/ 943-1301.** Reservations recommended. Men in tank tops are not allowed. Main courses lunch $7.95–11.95, dinner $17.95–$25.95. AE, MC, V. Summer 6pm–12am; winter 11:30am–2pm, 5:30pm–12am. SEAFOOD/STEAK.

Located in the historic Yacht Club, this is a popular spot for special occasions. The dining room has light green stucco walls and contrasting dark wood ceiling beams; the state record (1988) marlin is mounted on one wall, and wine racks cover another. There are several salads, including Caesar with their special homemade dressing and fresh Parmesan dusted atop. Fresh fish entrees include herb-crusted salmon in a Thai ginger broth, and flounder Monique, baked and topped with medallions of scallops in garlic tomato sauce. Among other choices are fried shrimp, panfried crab cakes, seafood pescatore (shrimp, scallops, and crab in tomato basil cream with linguini), a 14-ounce lobster tail, prime rib, filet mignon, lamb chops, and chicken justine, sautéed with garlic, tomatoes and artichokes in a pesto cream. Lunches include salads and lighter versions of several of the dinner offerings. The Yacht Club has the best wine list in the area, with international wines ranging from $20 to $500 per bottle.

4 Brazosport

50 miles S of Houston; 65 miles SE of Galveston; 185 miles NW of Corpus Christi

There's actually no such place as a city or town, or even a community called "Brazosport." The name refers to close to a dozen small communities in Brazoria County, and primarily southern Brazoria County, near the mouth of the Brazos River along the Gulf of Mexico. These towns, which have a combined population of about 90,000, include Clute, Freeport, Surfside Beach, Lake Jackson, Angleton, Quintana, West Columbia, and Brazoria. There's a pleasant small-town atmosphere here that, combined with the docks, fishing boats, and beaches, reminds us of the south shore of Long Island in the 1950s. Some critics put down the area for its admittedly somewhat ugly chemical plants and other manufacturing and refinery facilities—Dow Chemical, Phillips 66, and BASF Corporation have major divisions here—but the thousands of jobs these industries have created, plus outright donations from the companies, have made possible many of the museums and recreational opportunities that are to be enjoyed here.

While fishing and enjoying the area's 21 miles of beach are certainly major attractions, the area is world famous for its

Impressions

"Life is all the sweeter for having been so nearly lost."
—Minnie Floria, survivor of a hurricane that hit the
Texas coast on August 16, 1915, killing 275 people
and doing more than $50 million in damage.

bird watching—the annual Christmas bird count in the town
of Freeport often reports more species of birds seen in 1 day
than at any other location in the United States. There are several wildlife refuges in the area, and practically anywhere along
the shore will provide opportunities to see dozens, if not hundreds, of bird species. In addition, the Brazosport area has the
distinction of being the birthplace of Texas, the spot where the
first Anglo settlement was established in 1821. The winter climate is delightful, with daytime temperatures often in the 70s
and even 80s. Summers, however, are hot, with highs of about
100°F, and the coastal areas are subject to hurricanes from late
summer through fall.

ESSENTIALS
GETTING THERE

From Houston take Tex. 288 south about 45 miles to Angleton, the Brazoria County seat. Lake Jackson is another 10 miles
south on Tex. 288, and Bus. 288 leads from Angleton to Clute
(10 miles south). Tex. highways 332 and 288 intersect in Lake
Jackson, heading southeast around it and Clute and then
divide, 332 continuing southeast to Surfside Beach, and 288
heading south to Freeport and Quintana. Brazoria is just west
of Lake Jackson on Tex. 332. West Columbia is about 15 miles
west of Angleton on Tex. 35, and 8 miles north of Brazoria via
Tex. 36, which also connects Freeport to Brazoria.

The nearest commercial airports are in Houston (see chapter 3).

VISITOR INFORMATION

Although most of the towns in the Brazosport area have their
own chambers of commerce, and some have visitor centers,
you can get area-wide information from the **Southern Brazoria County Visitors Convention Bureau,** 1239 W. Tex. 332,
Clute, TX 77531 (☎ **800/938-4853** or 979/265-2508;

fax 979/265-3535; www.tourist-info.org; e-mail: jscott@
computron.net); and the **Brazosport Convention & Visitors
Council,** 420 Tex. 332 West, Brazosport (Clute), TX 77531
(☎ **888/477-2505** or 979/265-2505; fax 979/265-4246;
www.tourtexas.com/brazosport; e-mail bcvc@tgn.net). Both
organizations operate visitor centers.

GETTING AROUND

The only practical way to explore this area is by automobile,
either your own or a rental. The major roads are Tex. highways
288, 332, 35, and 36. Tex. 288/332 wraps around the west
and south sides of Lake Jackson and Clute, and this is where
many of the lodging facilities are located.

FAST FACTS

The **Brazosport Memorial Hospital,** 100 Medical Dr. (just off
Tex. 288), Lake Jackson (☎ **979/297-4411**), has a 24-hour
emergency room. **Clute's post office,** located at 530 E. Main
St., is open Monday through Friday from 7:30am to 5pm, Saturday from 10am to noon. The **Lake Jackson post office,**
located at 210 Oak Dr. South, is open Monday through Friday
from 8:30am to 5pm, Saturday from 10am to 2pm.

SPECIAL EVENTS

The **San Jacinto Festival & Texas History Day** takes place in
mid-April; the **Bird Migration Celebration** is held in late
April; the **Cinco de Mayo Celebration** is held in early May;
the **Fishing Fiesta Fishing Tournament** takes place from late
June to early July; the **Great Texas Mosquito Festival** is held
in late July; the **Brazoria County Fair** takes place in October;
the **Lake Jackson Festival of Lights** is in mid-November; and
the **Christmas Boat Parade** is held in December.

SPORTS & OUTDOOR PURSUITS

Bird watching, fishing, and hanging out on the beach are the
top outdoor activities in the Brazosport area.

BIRD WATCHING & WILDLIFE VIEWING   The Texas
Gulf Coast is renowned for its bird watching, and birders
come from around the world to try to catch a glimpse of
roseate spoonbills, black-necked stilts, crested caracaras, and
several hundred other species. Binoculars or cameras with tele-
photo lenses are especially helpful, and insect repellent is practically mandatory year-round.

There are several wildlife refuges in the Brazosport area. The most developed is the **Brazoria National Wildlife Refuge,** which covers 43,000 acres and was established to protect coastal wetlands for migratory birds and other wildlife. The Information Center, located near the entrance to the refuge, has interpretive panels on what you want to watch for, and a boardwalk outside the Information Center leads across wetlands, where you may spot an alligator. The boardwalk provides access to the ⅝-mile Big Slough Birding Trail, which loops through a stand of trees where you might see songbirds such as warblers and vireos, as well as sandhill cranes, snow geese, pintails, and mottled ducks. The refuge also has a 2-mile hiking and biking trail that follows an abandoned railway line and provides views across a terrain of prairie, where you might see more than a dozen species of sparrows, white-tailed hawks, and white-tailed kites. In addition, a 7-mile driving tour (a brochure is available at the Information Center) offers excellent opportunities to see a wide variety of birds and other wildlife, and also provides access to several observation decks. The refuge, which also allows fishing and hunting, is open daily from sunrise to sunset year-round, with free admission. To get to the refuge, take FM 523 north from Freeport or south from Angleton to CR 227, which you follow slightly more than 1½ miles northeast to the refuge entrance.

For information on Brazoria and other national wildlife refuges, contact the **Texas Mid-Coast National Wildlife Refuge Complex,** 1212 N. Velasco St., Suite 200, Angleton, TX 77515 (☎ **979/849-6062;** http://southwest.fws.gov).

In the community of Quintana the **Quintana Bird Sanctuary** is located on Lamar Street across from the Quintana Town Hall (☎ **979/233-0848**), which can provide a bird checklist and other information. The small, wooded preserve is open 24 hours a day with free admission. It attracts numerous migrating birds, as well as butterflies and small animals. It has a short loop trail (dirt) with strategically located benches. Nearby is a separate xeriscape garden.

FISHING   This area also offers excellent fishing for grouper, ling, amberjack, and red snapper—the state record 36.1-pound red snapper was caught in 1995 off the Freeport coast. Anglers can choose from among about a dozen charter-fishing boats, most based in Freeport Harbor. A variety of deep-sea fishing trips are offered, priced either per individual or for the entire boat. One company, **Captain Elliott's Party Boats** (☎ 979/233-1811; www.deep-sea-fishing.com), offers 12-hour deep-sea fishing trips (6am to 6pm) at $75 per adult weekends, $70 weekdays, and $45 for children 12 and under. Other companies we suggest contacting are **Action Charters** (☎ 979/233-2999), **David's Deep Sea Charters** (☎ 979/297-4410), and **Freeport Charter Boats** (☎ 800/605-5285). There are numerous places for shore, beach, pier, and jetty fishing, including Quintana and Surfside beaches and the Brazoria National Wildlife Refuge (see above). Those who brought a boat will find a number of public boat ramps—check with one of the visitor bureaus (see "Visitor Information," above) for locations.

BEACHCOMBING   Although the beaches here are far from pristine—they tend to be rocky and the sand is more brown than white—it's still fun to dig your toes into the cool sand, walk along the shore, build a sand castle, watch the freighters and shorebirds, and look for seashells among the stones. Driving is permitted on most beaches here, although we especially like the pedestrian-only 5th Street beach at **Quintana Beach County Park,** in the community of Quintana (☎ 800/872-7578 or 979/233-1461), which has a campground (see "Camping," below), good bird watching, a playground, horseshoe pits, and a picnic area, and charges a $4 per vehicle day-use fee.

MORE TO SEE & DO

Brazoria County Historical Museum. 100 E. Cedar St., just off Bus. 288, Angleton. ☎ **979/864-1208.** www.bchm.org. Free admission (donations welcome). Mon–Fri 9am–5pm, Sat 9am–3pm; closed major holidays.

A must-stop for anyone interested in the real Old West and the beginnings of Texas, this museum is located in the 1897 Brazoria County Courthouse, a restored structure that was built in the Italian Renaissance style popular in the late 1800s, and then "modernized" between 1913 and 1927. The Anglo influence that dominates Texas today began in Brazoria County in 1821, when Stephen F. Austin established a colony of 300 families at the mouth of the Brazos River. This museum's primary permanent exhibit does an excellent job of describing not only the colony, but also all the events since the arrival of the first Anglo settlers. The large exhibit, which contains 68 panels, replicas of the era's weapons and tools, and a variety of artifacts and documents, is located in the historic courtroom on the second floor (handicap accessible).

Most of the rest of the museum is devoted to changing exhibits that include historic subjects such as the courthouses of Texas and the Civil War's impact on the area. During our visit, we were especially impressed with an exhibit on the hurricanes that struck the Texas Gulf Coast in the early 1900s. The museum also has a well-stocked gift and bookshop and a research center that is an excellent source for those doing genealogical or other research on Brazoria County.

✪ **The Center for the Arts & Sciences.** 400 College Dr., Clute. ☎ **979/ 265-7661.** www.bcfas.org. E-mail: tcas@bcfas.org. Free admission to the museum, art gallery, and nature trail; planetarium $3 adults, $2 students and children. Theater and orchestra performances $8–$12. Museum and art gallery Tues–Sat 10am–5pm, Sun 2–5pm; closed major holidays. Planetarium shows Tues 7pm. Nature trail open daily dawn to dusk. From the intersection of Tex. hwys. 332 and 288 in Lake Jackson, head east on Oyster Creek Dr., through Lake Jackson and into Clute; Oyster Creek Dr,. becomes College Dr. after it crosses the railroad tracks in Clute. The Center is just ahead on the left, adjoining the campus of Brazosport College. In Clute, you can take Dixie Dr. north from Tex. 332/288 and turn right onto Oyster Creek Dr. From Bus. 288 turn west (right) directly onto College Dr. and the Center will be on your right after crossing the bridge over Oyster Creek.

One of those rare entities that does a whole lot of things very well, The Center for the Arts & Sciences is just what its name implies: a large center that includes a fine natural history museum, a small planetarium, an attractive art gallery, two theaters for a variety of performing arts events, and a nature trail. Under the wing of the Brazosport Fine Arts Council, the center is also home to a theater group, symphony orchestra, and the Brazosport Art League.

The **Brazosport Museum of Natural Science** has a collection of more than 14,000 seashells, and is credited with instigating the movement to make the lightning whelk the official State Shell of Texas, which occurred in 1987. Also, in its 12,000 square feet of floor space, are exhibits on archeology, fossils, dinosaurs, rocks and minerals (including a fluorescent mineral room), wildlife ranging from butterflies to an African elephant, bird watching, and a collection of jade and ivory carvings. The **Planetarium** has a 30-foot dome and lots of high-tech projection equipment to produce a variety of night sky experiences. It seats 72. A ¾-mile self-guided **nature trail** meanders through bottomland along Oyster Creek adjacent to the center.

The center's **art gallery,** under the direction of the Brazosport Art League, presents nine exhibits each year, ranging from local artists to national shows. The exhibits, which change every 4 to 6 weeks, open with a Saturday evening reception, at which the artists are usually present, and refreshments are served. The works are often for sale. In addition, music recitals in the gallery, and art classes and workshops are periodically offered in the adjacent studio. Contact the center offices for the current schedule.

There are two modern, well-designed theaters in the center; the proscenium theater seats 391, and the arena theater, which sometimes presents theater-in-the-round, seats from 150 to 199, depending on how it's set up. **Brazosport Center Stages,** the longest-running continuously operating theater group in Texas (it began in 1943), presents about a half dozen productions each year. The **Brazosport Symphony Orchestra** presents a variety of concerts ranging from classical to pop during its September-to-May season, with a combination of local musicians and guest artists. In addition, every other year (in even-numbered years) the center stages, as a fundraiser, an **Elizabethan Madrigal Feast,** in full costume, on the first 2 weekends in December.

Lake Jackson Historical Museum. 249 Circle Way, Lake Jackson. ☎ **979/ 297-1570.** www.lakejacksonmuseum.org. Admission $3 adults, $2.50 seniors, $1 youths ages 8–18, children under 8 free. Tues–Sat 10am–4pm, Sun 1–5pm; closed major holidays. From Tex. 322/288 turn east onto This Way and take the first right onto Circle Way; the museum will be on your left.

This impressive museum has its focus on the history of the Brazosport area, and particularly the community of Lake Jackson, but don't write it off as another one of those dusty little museums containing relics from local residents' attics. This is a modern, extremely well-executed museum that has some fascinating exhibits, even if you don't give a hoot about Lake Jackson. Actually, Dow Chemical Company created the community of Lake Jackson during World War II because workers at the company's new Texas facilities needed somewhere to live. So this historical museum is very much a "modern" historical museum that devotes much of its 12,000 square feet to

The Great Texas Mosquito Festival

What do you do in a popular tourist destination when the mosquitoes come out in full force? Follow the lead of the fun-loving folks in Clute, Texas, and throw a party dedicated to this delightful little bloodsucker. The Great Texas Mosquito Festival, which began in 1981, takes place the last Thursday, Friday, and Saturday of each July, offering carnival rides, games, races, way too much food, arts and crafts sales, and generally a good time for all. There's dancing to live music by top country, rock, Tejano, and R&B groups, plus barbecue and fajitas cook-offs, a horseshoe-pitching tournament, haystack dives, bike and skate tours, and a disc golf tournament. Specialty contests—perhaps the highlights of the festival—include the Mosquito Legs competition, the Mosquito Calling contest, the Senior Citizen Mosquito Swatter contest, and the ever-popular Ms. Quito Beauty Pageant. For more information, contact the **Clute Parks and Recreation Department** (☎ **800/371-2971** or 979/ 265-8392), or the **Southern Brazoria County Visitors Convention Bureau** (see "Visitor Information," above). And don't forget your insect repellent.

Dow Chemical and its executives and scientists, although there are also displays on the area's earlier American Indian and pioneer days.

Among our favorite exhibits here are the *Windecker Eagle,* a revolutionary airplane constructed of composite materials with help from Dow Chemical scientists that is invisible to radar, and is considered the predecessor to the *Stealth Fighter.* There's also a *Windecker Eagle* flight simulator you can try out, two eerily lifelike animatrons (Aldon Dow and a Dow Chemical executive), a typical 1940s living room with a radio blaring 1940s music, a theater that shows films of the Lake Jackson area from the 1940s, and a number of interactive exhibits for kids. The museum is on two floors, with an elevator.

Sea Center Texas. 300 Medical Dr., Lake Jackson. ☎ **979/292-0100.** www. tpwd.state.tx.us/fish/hatch/seacenter.htm. Free admission (donations welcome). Tues–Fri 9am–4pm, Sat 10am–5pm, Sun 1–4pm; closed major holidays. From Tex. 332/288 turn west onto Plantation Dr. to Medical Dr., turn north (right), then follow the signs.

A 50,000-gallon aquarium containing marine life of the Texas Gulf Coast, such as Gordon, the 250-pound grouper, is the centerpiece of the exhibits in the Sea Center Texas visitor center, where you'll also see sharks up to 12 feet long and a variety of other open water species. There are also tanks with exhibits on other types of marine environments, including salt marshes, reefs, and a coastal bay, with appropriate fish. A shallow Touch Pool contains blue crabs, hermit crabs, snails, urchins, and other marine creatures that can be handled (if that's something you want to do). Outside the visitor center is a 5-acre wetlands with elevated boardwalks and signs discussing the numerous birds and other wildlife you might encounter there. A free nature checklist is available in the visitor center. There's also a hatchery on the grounds, with high-tech life support systems for species such as the spotted sea trout, and brood fish tanks to produce larvae that is used to stock some of the center's 35 acres of ponds.

WHERE TO STAY
HOTELS, MOTELS, & BED AND BREAKFASTS

Among the national chain motels in the Brazosport area is our favorite, the ✪ **La Quinta Inn,** 1126 Tex. 332 West, Clute (☎ **800/531-5900** or 979/265-7461), with spacious, very attractive rooms, and rates for two of $58 to $82. Other reliable chains include the **Comfort Suites,** 296 Abner Jackson Pkwy., Lake Jackson (☎ **800/228-5150** or 979/297-5545), with rates of $85 to $125 double; **Days Inn,** 805 Tex. 332 West, Clute (☎ **800/329-7466** or 979/265-3301) which charges $46 to $60 double; **Holiday Inn Express,** 809 Tex. 332 West, Clute (☎ **800/465-4329** or 979/265-5252), with rates for two of $64 to $79; **Motel 6,** 1000 Tex. 332, Clute (☎ **800/466-8536** or 979/265-4764), charging $36 for two; and **Ramada Inn,** 925 Tex. 332, Lake Jackson (☎ **800/272-6232** or 979/297-1161), charging $90 to $155 double. There's also another **Days Inn,** at 1809 N. Velasco, Angleton (☎ **800/329-7466** or 979/849-5822), with rates for two of $61 to $71. Tax adds about 13% to lodging bills unless otherwise noted.

✪ **Roses & the River.** 7074 County Rd., 506, Brazoria, TX 77422. ☎ **800/610-1070** or 979/798-1070. Fax 979/798-1070. www.roses-and-the-river. com. E-mail: hosack@www.roses-and-the-river.com. 3 units. A/C TV TEL. $125 double (tax included). Rates include full breakfast. AE, DISC, MC, V. Suitable for children 12 and older. From Brazoria, go southwest on Tex. 521, cross the San Bernard River and take the first right turn, onto County Road 506. After about 1½ miles, you'll find Roses & the River on the right.

A delightful Texas farmhouse-style home in an idyllic setting is what you'll find at Roses & the River. This bed-and-breakfast inn sits on almost 3.5 acres along the San Bernard River, with trees and well-kept lawns and an abundance of beautiful rose bushes. Because of the warm Gulf Coast climate, the roses bloom year-round, although they're usually best in October and November. There are sitting areas along the river (and a dock for those who brought boats), plus a long veranda offering a peaceful and protected sitting area. Inside, the lobby/living room has a fireplace with comfortable seating and a separate dining room where the homemade breakfasts are served. There are three guest rooms, all on the second floor (no elevator), that are Rose themed and appropriately colored, somewhat elegant yet cheerful and inviting. Each of the spacious rooms has a full private bathroom (one with a fantastic clawfooted spa tub), one queen bed, and a TV with a VCR (movies available for free use). Guest rooms contain a few antiques, but mostly contemporary furnishings. Two rooms have views of the river, and the third overlooks the rose garden. Innkeepers Mary Jo and Dick Hosack plan to build another house with five or six more rooms in 2002. Smoking is permitted outside only.

Surfside Motel. 330 Coral Ct., Surfside Beach, TX 77541. ☎ **979/233-4585.** 17 units. A/C TV TEL. $60 double, kitchenette units $90 up to 5 people. AE, DISC, MC, V. Pets accepted. As you come into Surfside Beach on Tex. 332, you come to a traffic light, turn northeast (left) onto Bluewater Highway to Coral Court.

Of the several independent motels in the community of Surfside Beach, we particularly like this one, which is nothing fancy but offers clean, well-maintained rooms at very reasonable rates. Although you can't quite see the beach, it's an easy walk at just 100 yards away. You've got two room choices at the Surfside Motel, both being simply decorated with white stucco walls. The standard rooms are a bit small, with one nice, firm queen-sized bed, a microwave and small refrigerator (coffeemakers available by request), and a bathroom with shower only. About half the units are kitchenettes, each with two queens and one twin bed, a fully equipped kitchen, and a full bathroom with a shower/tub combo. Guests have use of a sundeck, picnic tables, barbecue grills, and horseshoe pits.

CAMPING

Our choice for camping in this area is the Brazoria County–run **Quintana Beach County Park,** 5th Street, in the community of Quintana. Practically on the water, this campground has fairly close sites, but there are some low palm trees and lots of grass, and it's a very short walk to the beach. There are 56 sites (including 19 pull-through RV sites), and a small group of grassy "tent only" sites. The campground has paved roads, showers, a self-serve laundry, an RV dump station, picnic tables, grills, a playground, and horseshoe pits. Boardwalks lead from the campground among several weathered wood buildings to the beach. Camping rates from May through September are $18 to $20 for water, sewer, and electric hook-ups, $18 for water and electric, and $15 for no hook-ups. From October through April, rates are $17 to $18 for full hook-ups, $16 for water and electric, and $12 for no hook-ups. Day-use costs $4 per vehicle. Information is available by calling ☎ **800/872-7578** or 979/233-1461. From Tex. 36/288 in Freeport, turn right onto FM 1495, and after crossing the Intercoastal Waterway on a swing bridge, turn left onto Quintana Road, which becomes Lamar Street in Quintana. Turn right on 8th Street, then left on Burnett Street to 5th Street.

Those who don't mind roughing it can also drive onto and camp for free on most parts of Quintana Beach (ask for details at the RV park or at area visitor centers).

WHERE TO DINE

✪ **Café Annice.** 24 Circle Way, Lake Jackson. ☎ **979/292-0060.** Reservations accepted for large parties only. Main courses lunch $5.50–$8.95, dinner $9.95–$19.95. AE, DISC, MC, V. Mon–Fri 11am–2pm, Sat 10am–2:30pm, Mon–Thurs 5–9pm, Fri–Sat 5–10pm. Closed Thanksgiving and Christmas. From Tex. 332/288, turn northeast onto This Way, take the first left onto Circle Way and follow it around to downtown. CONTINENTAL.

There's a decidedly uptown feel to this casual modern restaurant that is a favorite of local businesspeople, and, in our estimation, borders on fine dining for both lunch and dinner. Modern art decorates the light-colored brick walls, and the high ceiling makes the dining room appear larger than it really is. Lunch choices include a variety of innovative sandwiches, such as the

Caesar wrap—chicken breast, romaine lettuce, carrots, red onions, plum tomatoes, and a homemade Caesar spread, wrapped in a roasted garlic and herb tortilla. Dinner entrees feature tempting selections of seafood, Angus beef, and chicken, including the excellent chicken Annice, which is breaded chicken topped with mushrooms, artichokes, plum tomatoes, and capers, sautéed with Marsala wine and served with grilled vegetable ragout and garlic mashed potatoes. A number of pasta specialties are served for both lunch and dinner, including the delightful grilled chicken fettuccine, with peas and mushrooms in a creamy Alfredo sauce. Among the more than a dozen fresh-baked desserts, we heartily recommend the Italian cream cake.

DJ's BBQ. 906 W. Plantation Dr., Clute. ☎ **979/265-6331.** Reservations not accepted. Main courses $2.90–$6.50. AE, DISC, MC, V. Mon 11am–3pm, Tues–Sat 11am–8pm. Just off Dixie Dr. on the left side of Plantation. BARBECUE.

A visit to Texas is not complete without at least one meal of genuine Texas barbecue, and in the Brazosport area, DJ's is the place to go. Plates and sandwiches are available to eat in or take out, and you can also buy the tender, slow-roasted beef brisket, pork, turkey, sausage, ham, or chicken in bulk, starting at $1.50 to $1.80 for a quarter pound, or $2 for a quarter chicken. The lunch and dinner plates include your choice of one, two, or three meats plus a choice of two of the following: potato salad, pinto beans, corn, coleslaw, or green beans. This is a down-home, casual type of place—to say it's unpretentious would be an understatement—with food served cafeteria-style in a dining room decorated with ranching tools and hardware, picnic table seating, and disposable utensils. Naturally, there's a country-music radio station playing in the background.

The Jetties. 104 2nd St., Quintana. ☎ **979/373-9730.** Main courses lunch $3.75–$9.95, dinner $3.75–$16.95. No credit cards. Sun–Thurs 10am–9pm, Fri–Sat 10am–10pm. From Tex. 36/288 in Freeport, turn right onto FM 1495, then left onto Quintana Rd, which becomes Lamar St. in Quintana. Turn right on 8th St., then left on Burnett St., right on 2nd. The Jetties is at the end of the road. AMERICAN.

We kept expecting to see singer Jimmy Buffett and a bunch of noisy beach bums burst into The Jetties during our visit. Well, Jimmy didn't make it, but at least the beach bums did, sandy feet and all. This is an ultracasual, friendly, funky beach hang-out, with a small dining room with great views of the Gulf, where you can watch the fishing boats and freighters chug by.

No Shoes, No Shirts, No Problems
    —Handwritten sign posted at the entrance to The Jetties,
         a beachfront restaurant on Quintana Beach.

There's also an outside deck and additional seating in the sand along the jetty. Surprisingly (at least we were surprised), the food is really good, from the half-pound burgers served with hand-cut french fries to the beer-batter-dipped shrimp, a favorite of the locals. Sandwiches, burgers, and baskets (such as fresh battered catfish served with hush puppies and tarter sauce) are served all the time, but dinners, such as grilled shrimp or a charcoal-grilled rib-eye steak topped with sautéed mushrooms and onions, is served only after 5pm. Service is a bit slow here, mostly because everything is prepared fresh as it's ordered, but The Jetties has such a friendly, happy atmosphere that nobody seems to care.

✪ **Red Snapper Inn.** 402 Bluewater Hwy., Surfside Beach. ☎ **979/239-3226.** Reservations accepted for large parties only. Main courses $4.95–$16.95. No credit cards. Mon–Fri 11am–2pm, 5–9pm; Sat–Sun 11am–9pm. As you enter Surfside Beach on Tex. 332, you come to a traffic light, turn northeast (left) onto Bluewater Hwy. The restaurant will be on your right a few blocks down. SEAFOOD.

What's the point in going to the Gulf if you're not going to indulge in fresh seafood? And it doesn't get any fresher and better than at the Red Snapper. Not surprisingly, the decor is nautical, with a large aquarium, a fishnet, beach flotsam, and a surfboard highlighting the somewhat upscale but still very casual dining room. Although the menu is primarily classic seafood such as shrimp sautéed with garlic and mushrooms and served with rice pilaf, or grilled boneless flounder stuffed with crabmeat dressing, you'll also find some exciting Greek and Cajun touches. We especially recommend the baked shrimp, with feta cheese and fresh tomatoes, and served with buttered spaghetti; and the sautéed fillet of snapper in a sauce of pulverized onions, oregano, lemon juice, and olive oil. Also a good bet are the oysters brochette, grilled bacon-wrapped oysters (not breaded) with meunière butter and served on rice pilaf. Nonseafood items include a charbroiled choice 14-ounce rib-eye steak, the very popular charbroiled Greek meatballs with spaghetti, and that Texas standard, chicken-fried steak with cream gravy.

5 Rockport

182 miles SW of Houston; 35 miles NE of Corpus Christi

If we were going to live on the Gulf Coast, it would be in picturesque Rockport, Texas. This is an absolutely delightful little town, with a good (although not great) public beach, wonderful opportunities for bird watching, boating, fishing, and other outdoor activities, and the best art scene of any of the small towns we've seen in southern and western Texas.

Rockport and its neighbor, Fulton, have a combined population of about 5,000, but are home to about 150 resident artists and a half-dozen or so commercial art galleries, in addition to the excellent Rockport Center for the Arts. Rancher George Ware Fulton established tiny Fulton in 1866, and the much larger Rockport emerged the following year as a seaport. Today the Rockport-Fulton area, along with Aransas Pass (12 miles south), is a major port for commercial and sport fishing, and is famous as the winter home for North America's largest flock of whooping cranes.

ESSENTIALS
GETTING THERE

Both Rockport and Fulton are along Tex. 35, which connects with U.S. 87 to the north and U.S. 181 to the south.

VISITOR INFORMATION

Contact the **Rockport-Fulton Area Chamber of Commerce,** 404 Broadway, Rockport, TX 78382 (☎ **800/826-6441** or 361/729-6445; www.rockport-fulton.org).

GETTING AROUND

Tex. 35 comes into town from the north and bends southwest to skirt Rockport's western edge, with Bus. 35 heading into downtown. Just north of downtown, Fulton Beach Road angles northeast off Bus. 35 to hug the coast. At Rockport Harbor Bus. 35 turns west away from the water and Austin Street continues south to FM 1069, which heads west, crossing Bus. 35, to connect with Tex. 35. FM 2165 runs north-south between Tex. 35 and Bus. 35.

FAST FACTS

The nearest full-service hospital, with a 24-hour emergency room, is **North Bay Hospital,** which is 11 miles south of Rockport at 1711 W. Wheeler Ave., Aransas Pass (☎ **361/ 758-8585**), and also provides 24-hour physician referrals (☎ **800/265-8624**). The **post office,** located at 1550 FM 2165 in Rockport, is open Monday through Friday from 9am to 4:30pm, Saturday from 9am to noon.

SPECIAL EVENTS

The **Fulton Oysterfest** takes place in early March; the **Texas State Kite Festival** is held in May; the **Rockport Art Festival** takes place in late June and/or early July; the **Hummer/Bird Celebration** is held in mid-September; **SeaFair** takes place during mid-October; and the **Celebration of Lights & Boat Parade** is staged in early December.

SPORTS & OUTDOOR PURSUITS

BIRD WATCHING & WILDLIFE VIEWING   This region is among the nation's premier bird-watching destinations, and the best spot for birding here is the ✪ **Aransas National Wildlife Refuge.** Although almost 400 species of birds have been seen at the refuge, it is famous as the main winter home for the near-extinct whooping crane, America's tallest bird, at 5 feet high with a 7-foot wingspan. In the 1930s there were only 15 whooping cranes known to exist in North America, but they are making a comeback, and now there are an estimated 400, more than half of which spend their winters—usually from November through April—at Aransas National Wildlife Refuge. They are sometimes also seen at nearby **Goose Island State Park** (see below). The whoopers spend the warmer months in Canada's Northwest Territories at Wood Buffalo National Park, about 2,400 miles north.

Other birds you're likely to see at the refuge include American white pelicans, great blue herons, great and snowy egrets, roseate spoonbills, mottled ducks, black and turkey vultures, American kestrels, northern bobwhites, western and least sandpipers, laughing gulls, Caspian terns, scissor-tailed fly-catchers, cliff swallows, northern mockingbirds, white-eyed vireos, northern cardinals, red-winged blackbirds, and eastern meadowlarks. Although late fall through spring is the best time to see birds, some, such as northern bobwhites, killdeer,

Impressions

"When we hear this call we hear no mere bird. He (the whooping crane) is the symbol of our untamable past."

—Naturalist Aldo Leopold

herons and egrets, mottled ducks, vultures, mourning doves, Carolina wrens, and vireos are year-round residents. April and May usually see large numbers of colorful songbirds.

In addition to birds, the refuge is home to a variety of frogs and other amphibians, about 30 species of snakes (about a half dozen are poisonous), turtles, lizards, and the refuge's largest reptile, the American alligator, which is often seen in summer when there is sufficient water to fill the freshwater ponds. Mammals commonly seen include white-tailed deer, javelina, wild boars, raccoons, eastern cottontail rabbits, and nine-banded armadillos. Also present but only occasionally seen are bobcats and opossums.

A 16-mile paved auto tour loop meanders through a variety of habitats, offering access to a 40-foot observation tower, a boardwalk that leads through a salt marsh to the coastline, and other viewing areas. The refuge has nine walking trails, ranging from 1/10 to 1½ miles, a picnic area, and also an impressive Wildlife Interpretive Center with information, exhibits, a bookstore, and administration offices. There are also seasons for hunting and saltwater fishing access. Camping is not permitted.

For information contact the **Aransas National Wildlife Refuge,** P.O. Box 100, Austwell, TX 77950 (☎ **361/286-3559;** http://southwest.fws.gov). It's located about 35 miles by road northeast of Rockport via Tex. 35, FM 774, and FM 2040. The refuge is open daily from just before sunrise to just after sunset, and the **Wildlife Interpretive Center** is open daily from 8:30am to 4:30pm. Admission to the refuge costs $5 per car. Binoculars are available to borrow at the Wildlife Interpretive Center. Insect repellent is recommended year-round.

As one of the best birding areas in North America, you'll generally find that whatever you're doing outdoors will be interrupted to look at birds, ranging from rare whooping cranes to colorful songbirds and rare neotropical species seldom seen in the United States. Among areas to go to see birds and other wildlife is the **Connie Hagar Cottage Sanctuary,** at First and Church streets in Rockport, which has trails and a self-guided tour on the property where well-known bird watcher Connie Hagar (1886–1973) and her husband lived. The grounds are open daily from sunrise to sunset, and admission is free. The Texas Department of Transportation's rest area on the east side of N. Tex. 35, south of Traylor Street, in Rockport, has a **Demonstration Bird Garden and Wetlands Pond** with a ⅘-mile interpretive nature trail. A good spot to see birds, especially hummingbirds, this rest area also has a pleasant picnic area. It's open 24 hours and admission is free. For information on both of these areas, plus maps and directions to other birding areas contact the Rockport-Fulton Area Chamber of Commerce (see "Visitor Information," above).

A number of companies offer **birding boat tours,** generally from November through March. Tours are in shallow draft boats and usually are 3 to 4 hours long. Costs ranges from $30 to $35 per person, with discounts for children and senior citizens, but several companies will take from 1 to 6 people for a flat rate of about $150. Some guarantee that you'll see whooping cranes. Among those that charge per person are **Captain John Howell** (☎ 800/245-9324 or 361/729-7525); **Captain Ray Little** (☎ 800/782-2473 or 361/729-4855); and **Captain Ted's Whooping Crane Tours** (☎ 800/338-4551 or 361/729-9589). Those offering the flat rate option for up to six people include **Captain Sally Ann Moffett** (☎ 361/729-9095) and **Friebele's Guide Service** (☎ 361/729-5676).

FISHING   In addition to birding, fishing is extremely popular here, and with very good reason—fishing's great for a variety of species including trout, croaker, flounder, sheepshead, and redfish in the bay and sailfish, marlin, tarpon, ling, king mackerel, grouper, and red snapper offshore. There are public fishing piers in Fulton Harbor and at Rockport Beach Park, as well as numerous other areas. There are more than three-dozen fishing guides in the Rockport, Fulton, and Port Aransas areas that offer bay and deep-sea fishing trips. Rates vary considerably, but can be as low as $25 per person for a half-day of bay fishing. Among those to contact are **Crystal Blue Charters** (☎ 800/920-0931 or 361/749-5904), **Deep Sea Headquarters** (☎ 361/749-5597), **Dolphin Dock** (☎ 800/393-3474; www.dolphindock.com), **Fish On Guide Service** (☎ 361/729-4244), and **Woody's Sport Center** (☎ 800/211-9227 or 361/749-6969). For additional information on where to fish from shore or for a complete list of area fishing guides, check with the Rockport-Fulton Area Chamber of Commerce (see "Visitor Information," above).

Anglers and birders especially like **Goose Island State Park** (☎ **361/729-2858**), which not only is a good spot to see the endangered whooping crane but also is home to The Big Tree, a giant live oak with seemingly countless twisting branches that is estimated to be more than 1,000 years old. It's more than 35 feet in circumference, 44 feet high, and has a crown spread of 89 feet. The park has an island section that is mostly grassland and marsh and a wooded mainland section. There's a short paved hiking and biking path, two playgrounds, picnic tables and grills, a boat ramp, and a 1,620-foot lighted fishing pier. Fish caught here include speckled trout, redfish, drum, flounder, and sheepshead, and crabbing and oystering are also popular. There are 102 campsites with water and electric hookups and 25 sites with water only, and the park also has restrooms with showers and an RV dump station. Entrance to the park costs $2 per person age 13 and older per day (free for children 12 and under), and camping costs an additional $8 to $13 per night, with reservations available (☎ **512/389-8900;** www.tpwd.state.tx.us). The park is about 12 miles from Rockport. Follow Tex. 35 north 10 miles to Park Road 13, which you follow 2 miles east to the park entrance.

BEACHCOMBING   One of our favorite beaches along the Gulf is at ✪ **Mustang Island State Park** (☎ **361/ 749-5246**), which has more than 5 miles of wide, sandy beach, with fine sand, few rocks and broken shells, and almost enough waves for surfing. A barrier island, Mustang Island offers excellent fishing from jetties, a swimming beach with a bathhouse, picnic tables with sun shelters, and good bird watching for pelicans, terns, gulls, and other permanent residents, plus migratory species in spring and fall. There is a campground that looks like a parking lot; it has 48 sites with water and electric hook-ups ($12 per night, with reservations ☎ **512/389-8900;** www.tpwd.state.tex.us), showers, and an RV dump station; and there is also almost unlimited beach camping (with no hook-ups) at $7 per night. Campers and day users age 13 and older must also pay the $3 per person day-use fee (no fee for children 12 and under). Day-use hours

Texas Trail Is for the Birders

The first of its kind in the nation, the **Great Texas Coastal Birding Trail** was completed in the spring of 2000, and pinpoints 308 birding sites along and near the 624 miles of Texas coastline. Using three colorful maps—covering the upper, middle, and lower portions of the coast—birders can locate the bird-watching sites, which are marked in the field with brown signs featuring the image of a black skimmer. The sites are all within an hour of each other (some much closer), and the maps contain detailed directions to each site, information about which particular species to look for, local contacts, and other information. With over 450 different species known to have been seen along the Texas coast, this is one of the prime birding areas of the country, with fall and winter usually the best times to see the most species. Copies of the birding maps are free at chambers of commerce, convention and visitors bureaus, state parks, wildlife refuges, and at Texas Travel Information Centers; and they can also be obtained by calling ☎ **888/TXBIRDS,** or contacting the **Texas Parks and Wildlife Department,** 4200 Smith School Rd., Austin, TX 78744-3291 (☎ **800/792-1112;** www.tpwd.state. tx.us/birdingtrails).

are 7am to 10pm. The park is one of the most popular of Texas state parks and is especially busy on summer weekends. Mustang Island is connected to Corpus Christi by a bridge and causeway at the south end and to Aransas Pass via a free ferry on the north end.

You'll find a pleasant beach, with picnic tables, restrooms, and a pavilion at **Rockport Beach Park** (☎ 361/729-2213). The thin mile-long strip of beach is sandy, although a little rough with stones and broken shells, and during a November visit there were quite a few jellyfish. Beach parking costs $3 per day or $7 for a one-year pass.

MORE TO SEE & DO

Fulton Mansion State Historical Park. 317 Fulton Beach Rd. at Henderson St., Fulton. ☎ **361/729-0386.** Admission (including guided tour) $4 adults, $2 students age 6 through college seniors, free for children under 6. Tours Wed–Sun 9, 10, and 11am and 1, 2, and 3pm.

An absolute marvel when it was built in the 1870s, this luxurious six-bedroom five-story (including the basement) home not only was built to withstand hurricanes, but it had practically unheard of amenities for the day. These included a gas plant to provide fuel for interior lighting, a central hot-air heating system that boasted a cast-iron furnace in the basement with ducts leading to attractive fake fireplaces throughout the house, a hot-air laundry-drying system, and a gravity-fed water supply that provided water for bathtubs and toilets. There was also a water circulation system to cool perishable food and a dumbwaiter to transport food from the kitchen to the butler's pantry by the dining room. Built in the French Second Empire style that was popular among the wealthy of that era, the mansion has a slate mansard roof and interior woodwork on the first two floors is cypress with walnut trim.

The house was built by George and Harriet Fulton—he was an engineer, machinist, and cattle rancher—and was restored by Texas Parks & Wildlife. The mansion is furnished as it would have been in the 1870s and 1880s, and includes some of the family's original pieces. It can be seen only on guided tours, in which guides escort visitors through the several stories of the home (there is no elevator) and discuss its construction, furnishings, and especially the Fulton Family. Those touring the Fulton Mansion are asked to wear flat, soft-soled shoes to protect the floors and rugs.

✪ **Rockport Center for the Arts.** 902 Navigation Circle, Rockport. ☎ **361/729-5519.** Free admission. Tues–Sat 10am–4pm, Sun 1–4pm.

Several attractive art galleries and a delightful outdoor sculpture garden that was being developed during our visit make the Rockport Center for the Arts a top attraction for those who enjoy art. The Main Gallery presents about ten changing exhibits each year that range from local to international artists, with a variety of themes and mediums. There are often displays of students' work, and sometimes hands-on exhibits, in the Garden Gallery; and the Members Gallery presents an eclectic selection of works by members of the Rockport Art Association, which manages the center. Although subject matter varies considerably, there are often a number of sea and harbor scenes and paintings and drawings of birds—we especially enjoyed some of the watercolors of docks, boats, and pelicans in the

Members Gallery. Each of the gallery shows opens with a public reception, at which many of the artists are present, and works are often for sale. The Rockport Art Association sponsors the Rockport Art Festival each summer, in late June and/or early July; and also sponsors a series of art classes, workshops, and concerts (call for the current schedule).

Texas Maritime Museum. 1202 Navigation Circle, Rockport. ☎ **361/ 729-1271.** www.texasmaritimemuseum.org. E-mail: tmm@2fords.net. Admission $4 adults, $2 children ages 5–12, free for children 4 and under. Tues–Sat 10am–4pm, Sun 1–4pm. Closed major holidays.

From pirates to shipbuilding to offshore oil drilling, this excellent museum brings to life the story of the Texas Gulf Coast, with lots of hands-on exhibits, historic fishing gear and old strange-looking outboard motors. Among its changing and permanent exhibits you'll see artwork, such as the "Lighthouses of Texas" watercolors by Harold Phenix, a life-size ship's bridge where you can imagine yourself on the high seas, and even a small pirate ship. On the museum grounds are a survival capsule (used to escape offshore oil rigs in case of emergency), a 26-foot-long lifeboat, and a replica of a scow sloop fishing boat. The museum sponsors various events, such as the annual Festival of Wines on Memorial Day weekend, and from November through April offers a free lecture series (call for details).

WHERE TO STAY
HOTELS, MOTELS, & BED AND BREAKFASTS

Among the national chain motels in the Rockport and Fulton areas are the **Best Western Inn by the Bay,** 3902 N. Tex. 35, Fulton (☎ **800/235-6076** or 361/729-8351), with rates for two of $66 to $76; **Days Inn,** 1212 E. Laurel St. (at Tex. 35), Rockport (☎ **800/329-7466** or 361/729-6379), with rates for two of $55 to $85; and **Holiday Inn Express,** 301 N. Tex. 35, Rockport (☎ **888/727-2566** or 361/727-0283), with rates for two of $65 to $88.

Village Inn Motel. 503 N. Austin St., Rockport, TX 78382. ☎ **800/ 338-7539** for reservations, or ☎ **361/729-6370.** 26 units. A/C TV TEL. Summer $52–$55 double, $55–$75 suite and kitchenette units; winter $48–$52 double, $52–$68 suite and kitchenette units. Year-round $85–$95 full kitchen units. AE, DC, DISC, MC, V. Pets accepted for $10 per pet per day.

This extremely well-maintained two-story older motel—some parts are pre-1930—is an excellent choice for those seeking economical, comfortable lodging within walking distance of Rockport's beach, piers, attractions, and restaurants. Inside the bright yellow wood exterior are a wide variety of simply but attractively decorated units. The rooms are larger than average, with modern furnishings and from one to four beds. Four of the standard rooms have small refrigerators and microwaves; there are also suites, kitchenette units, and several units with full kitchens. Twelve units have shower only; the rest have shower/tub combos. There's an attractive outdoor swimming pool and tree-shaded lawn, and a self-serve laundry.

CAMPING

There are several dozen commercial campgrounds and RV parks in the Rockport area, plus camping at several nearby state parks (see "Bird Watching & Wildlife Viewing," above). Among those we recommend are **Ancient Oaks RV Park,** 1222 S. Tex. 35, Rockport (☎ **800/962-6134** for reservations, or ☎ **361/729-5051**), which has grassy sites shaded by oak trees, and rates of $22 per night; **Lagoons RV Resort,** 600 Enterprise Rd., Rockport (☎ **361/729-7834**), a large RV park with nice landscaping and rates of $20 to $24 per night; and **Rockport 35 RV Park,** 4851 N. Tex. 35, Rockport (☎ **800/392-2930** for reservations, or ☎ **361/729-2307;** www.rv35.com), which is mostly open and has recreation and exercise facilities and charges $20 to $22 per night. Most RV parks here offer weekly and monthly rates, in addition to nightly rates, to attract the "winter Texans."

WHERE TO DINE

The Big Fisherman. Tex. 188 (off Tex. 35) between Rockport and Aransas Pass. ☎ **361/729-1997.** Main courses $3.95–$21.95. AE, DISC, MC, V. Daily 11am–9pm or later. SEAFOOD/STEAK/CHICKEN.

Dark, noisy, and big, this popular restaurant is not the best choice for a romantic evening, but it's definitely the place to come when you want a lot of good food at very reasonable prices. The large, open dining room surrounds the kitchen, and although the restaurant is in a metal building, it's disguised fairly well with lattice work, indoor trees, and numerous neon beer advertising signs in the bar area. Illumination is from hanging single-bulb warehouse-style lights, and seating is at booths, tables for four, and long banquet-style tables with benches. Lunch specials ($5.95) are offered daily from 11am to 4pm, but most hungry folks come here for one of the

Texas's Most Deserted Beach

Those seeking an escape from civilization will find a long, picturesque beach with an abundance of birds and other wildlife, excellent fishing, but little else at **Matagorda Island State Park** (☎ **361/983-2215**). Located about 7 water miles south of the community of Port O'Connor, Matagorda Island is accessible only by boat—your own, a charter, or the park-operated passenger ferry that runs between the island and Port O'Connor. Private motor vehicles are not permitted on the island, but the park operates a shuttle service from the boat docks to the beaches. Visitors also can take mountain bikes to the island.

Once there, you'll find a narrow 38-mile-long island that has practically no development. A variety of guided tours are offered, in which you'll get to see whooping cranes and other birds, go beachcombing, examine the marine ecosystem, or see some of the island's historic sites, such as an 1852 lighthouse. Tours are usually from 6 to 9 hours. Most tours cost $8 for adults and $4 for children age 12 and under; whooping crane boat tours cost

all-you-can-eat platters, such as fried oysters, fried fish, Cajun fried crawfish tails, fried chicken, chicken fried steak, or filet mignon. There are also lesser-priced, not all-you-can-eat, versions of the above, plus a wide variety of other seafood, steak, and chicken dishes. Although most items here are fried, those seeking more heart-healthy selections have several choices, including Cajun grilled boneless chicken breast, Cajun boiled shrimp and crab legs, and grilled or broiled catch of the day.

Panjo's. 2744 N. Tex. 35 (in the Harbor Oaks Village Shopping Center), Rockport. ☎ **361/729-1411.** Main courses $3.95–$9.95; pizzas $3.25–$14.75. AE, DISC, MC, V. Mon–Thurs 11am–9pm, Fri–Sat 11am–10pm. PIZZA/PASTA/BURGERS.

Great pizza plus a variety of burgers, pastas, and other selections make Panjo's a good choice for either a tasty lunch or casual dinner. The atmosphere here is store-front pizza parlor, with solid wood and Formica tables, ceiling fans, and hand-painted wooden signs advertising local businesses, as well as warnings such as "Please don't throw pepperoni at the band."

$20 for adults and $15 for children 12 and under and include transportation from Port O'Connor to Matagorda Island.

Anglers catch flounder, mackerel, redfish, and spotted trout, among other species. In addition to the numerous birds to be seen on the island, those interested in wildlife should also watch for alligators, white-tailed deer, raccoons, coyotes, and jackrabbits. In all, there are about 80 miles of beach, dirt roads, and paths available for hiking and mountain biking.

Primitive campsites on the beach cost $4 per night, and a rustic bunkhouse has 22 beds with linens, plus restrooms and a common kitchen ($15 per person per night). An outdoor cold-water rinse is available near the docks. The passenger ferry runs a limited schedule from Thursday through Sunday plus holidays, and charges $10 for adults and $5 for children age 12 and under. Use of the island shuttle is free for those who arrive by ferry; for those who travel to the island by private or charter boat, the shuttle costs $2 for adults and $1 for children 12 and under. For ferry times and reservations call the park office (see above).

In pizza parlor style, you order at a counter and servers deliver your food. The pizzas come in sizes from mini to large, with a nice, crisp crust, and your choice of more than a dozen toppings. There are also eight varieties of charbroiled burgers, pasta selections such as chicken or shrimp Alfredo and primavera, and dinner plates including the shrimp kabob—charbroiled shrimp served on a bed of fettuccine with olive oil, garlic, and mushrooms. In addition, Panjo's offers several salads, including a tossed or dinner salad with especially good vinaigrette dressing. Delivery is available after 5pm.

Salad Works. 2841 N. Tex. 35 (in Live Oak Plaza), Rockport. ☎ **361/ 727-1105.** Main courses $2.50–$5.95. MC, V. Mon–Sat 11am–2pm, in winter open until 7pm Fri–Sat. SALAD/POTATO.

For some of the healthiest food you'll find in a state where the motto seems to be "If it ain't deep fried, it ain't worth eatin'," come to Salad Works. Not only is there an all-you-can-eat salad bar with more than 60 super-fresh items, but there's also homemade soup, chili, and some of the finest pinto beans and cornbread in the area. Then there's the potato section—Idaho potatoes, over one pound each, are stuffed with everything from Italian meatballs with spaghetti sauce and mozzarella cheese, to grilled chicken breast, sour cream, cheddar and Monterey cheeses, salsa, and guacamole. Or, take your spud to the potato bar and add whatever toppings you want. During our visit, plans were underway to add subs, grilled chicken breast, Philly steak, and other sandwiches. The decor in this busy storefront is light and open, with wood tables and chairs and decorations such as a birdhouse, painted milk can, pottery, and native Texas flowers adding a country atmosphere. The entire restaurant is non-smoking.

See also Accommodations and Restaurant indexes, below.

NOTES